Meeting the Challenge of

PARENTING
IN THE WEST

AN ISLAMIC PERSPECTIVE

D1051646

Meeting the Challenge of

PARENTING IN THE WEST

An Islamic Perspective

Dr. Ekram & Dr. Mohamed Rida Beshir

ENLARGED
FOURTH EDITION

amana publications

First Edition
(1998 A.C./1419 A.H.)

Second Edition
(2000A.C./1420 A.H.)

Third Edition
(2003 A.C./1424 A.H.)
Reprint
(2006 A.C./1427 A.H.)

Fourth Edition
(2009 A.C./1430 A.H.)
Reprint
(2018 A.C./1439 A.H.)

Library of Congress Cataloging-in-Publication Data

Beshir, Ekram.
  Meeting the challenge of parenting in the West : an Islamic perspective
/ Ekram & Mohamed Rida Beshir.
    p.cm. 23
  ISBN 0-915957-87-6
  1. Child rearing–Religious aspects–Islam. 2. Parenting–Religious aspects-
-Islam. 3. Muslim children–Religious life–Europe. I. Beshir, Mohamed Rida.
II. Title.
HQ769.3.B47 1998
649'.1'0882971–dc21   98–35846
                                                                      CIP

CONTENTS

ACKNOWLEDGMENTS

We wish to express deep appreciation for the contribution of both sister Khadija Haffaji and brother Zulf Khalfan for all the time they spent reviewing and editing this book. May Allah reward them with the best rewards.

We would also like to thank our children for their help formulating some of the case studies and practical examples. Their understanding and support are highly appreciated. We recognize that the time spent in writing this book was precious time that we could have spent with our children, however, because of our children's maturity, they themselves encouraged us to do this project for the benefit of Muslims in North America. May Allah reward them and all the dedicated Muslim boys and girls who struggle in the path of truth.

Dr. Ekram and Dr. Mohamed Rida Beshir

FOREWORD

I cannot remember ever having enjoyed a book—other than the Qur'an and Hadīth books—as much as I enjoyed reading *Meeting the Challenge of Parenting in the West: An Islamic Perspective* by Dr. Ekram and Dr. Mohamed Rida Beshir. I speak as a happily married husband for over one-third of a century, as a father of four daughters, and as a grandfather of eight grandsons. There are many things to be said about this book. First, it is fun to read. Second, it offers a wealth of knowledge about Islam and human relationships. Third, it provides extremely relevant and vital information in simple language that makes a great deal of sense.

This small volume touches the mind and the heart of the reader. It is essential, not only for parents, but for anyone who deals with human beings. I feel that this book should be required reading for young men and women who plan to get married, for counselors of all types and specialties, and for any professional who relies on effective relationships with people for professional success. It should also be required reading in premarital counseling, in any parenting program, and in any continued marital education.

Meeting the Challenge of Parenting in the West: An Islamic Perspective fulfills a great need at a level far beyond my expectations. One of the many beauties of the book is the real life model of the authors' family that reflects, proves, and augments the educational material contained therein. May Allah bless and reward the Beshir family for such a wonderful contribution.

Ahmed Elkadi
September 23, 1997
Panama City, Florida

PREFACE

To our beloved children: Amirah, Hoda, Noha, and Sumaiya, because of whom we hope Allah will have mercy on us and admit us into paradise.

To those who recognize the commitment and pursue the journey of parenthood; to those who recall the endless hours of bedtime stories, 'Id shopping, clothes wars, explanations of Santa's falsehood, and the showers from the wuḍū'-training years; to those who share our dream of one day seeing our babies stand strong against the wind of brainwashing greed and worldly evil by means of the goodness radiated by the light of Islam, this book is a map which includes every twist and turn on the road to the successful upbringing of children. It is the map that, with Allah's will, can show parents and their children the road to Heaven.

INTRODUCTION

In the 1960s and 1970s, Muslims in North America directed their attention to building mosques. From the late 1970s until now, they have been concerned primarily, and rightfully so, with establishing Islamic schools and secondarily with financial institutions.

These activities are part of the continuous, restless efforts of Muslims to ensure their healthy existence as a minority within North America and to guarantee the continuation of Islam as the religion of their offspring. However, these noble goals cannot be achieved without emphasizing children's *tarbiyah*, that is, education.

Tarbiyah is an important concept and refers to much more than "formal" education. Actually, it is teaching the art of dealing properly with human nature at various levels and in different situations, thus ensuring a person's balanced upbringing that fulfills the purpose of his or her creation as stipulated by Allah in the *Qur'an*.

وَإِذْ قَالَ رَبُّكَ لِلْمَلَائِكَةِ إِنِّي جَاعِلٌ فِي الْأَرْضِ خَلِيفَةً

Behold, your Lord said to the angels: I will create a vicegerent on earth. (2:30)

وَمَا خَلَقْتُ الْجِنَّ وَالْإِنْسَ إِلَّا لِيَعْبُدُونِ

I have not created the jinns and human beings to any end other than that they may know and worship Me. (51:56)

Successful *tarbiyah* can be achieved when it is based on Qur'anic guidance and the teachings of the Prophet Muhammad, may the most perfect of blessings and peace be upon him. Although Islamic schools can play an important role in the *tarbiyah* process, they alone cannot satisfy its requirements. The major responsibility continues to lie with parents. Children's *tarbiyah* should constitute the most important aspect of their lives. All parents should strive hard to teach themselves the art of Islamic *tarbiyah*. It should be considered an obligation, especially for parents who settle in North America. Without such an effort, generations of Muslim children could be lost to the North American "main stream."

It is quite encouraging to know that Islamic literature is rich with books on children's *tarbiyah* in different languages, particularly in Arabic. However, and without exception, the emphasis in these books is on basic theory and its principles. Often they lack practical implementation techniques and real life examples. Available literature is mainly written by scholars who never lived in North America and who have no first hand information on the type of pressures that minority children go through in this society. Although these books serve as references, North American Muslim parents will not find them helpful in the *tarbiyah* process. A comprehensive guide to *tarbiyah* is lacking.

The book in your hands fills the need for a practical guide to *tarbiyah*. As the authors, who have four children of our own all born and brought up in North America as proud Muslims, we feel at ease with ourselves and the society around us. We have a good knowledge of Islam, medicine, and child psychology and feel that we are (with the help of Allah) in a good position to pass our experiences on to other Muslim parents in North America. We pray to Allah that it will be beneficial and serve as a manual for their children's *tarbiyah* needs.

Worthy of note is that this book is not only for parents. The responsibility of children's *tarbiyah* does not start after the birth of a child. It starts much earlier than that, as the Prophet of Allah has emphasized, with the process of spouse selection. The Prophet said the following:

> A woman is married for four things, i.e., her wealth, her family status, her beauty, and her religion. So you should choose the religious one to attain success. (Bukhari)

This book is divided into eight chapters. The first chapter explains the objectives of *tarbiyah*. The second chapter describes the basic principles of *tarbiyah* deduced from *Qur'an* and the teachings of the Prophet Muhammad who was a *murabbi* (the person who conducts the *tarbiyah* process) and educator. The third chapter reflects on the present environment in North America, its importance and influence on children, and how parents can foster a positive environment with a strong support system for their children's development. In the fourth chapter, methods of *tarbiyah* are illustrated in detail with practical examples relevant to the North American situation. The fifth chapter is devoted to the discussions of common cases and problems which are usually faced by parents. Many case studies are described for various ages and genders. The reader is asked to analyze these cases and answer certain questions, thus, helping the reader to put the principles learned in previous sections into practice. Chapter six deals with the same case studies presented in chapter five, but for each case we explain the reason for the problem, the symptoms of the problem, and then suggest proper solutions. Chapter seven is something different. It is completely written by our four children. In it they describe their experience, their feelings, the way they deal with each other and the result of our work with them. You will sample some of their short stories and poetry at various stages of their life. Finally, chapter eight, lists additional tips for parents to remember at odd times when they are with their children.

The urgent need for developing children properly has even been recognized by officials of the dominant culture of North America who see the situation as an impending disaster. To illustrate where today's society stands regarding the upbringing of children and instilling ethics, morality and responsibility, we quote the following from the editorial page of the newspaper *USA Today* under the heading "The Debate: Values in School." In it Ronald Reagan is quoted as having said: "We don't expect children to discover the principles of calculus on their own, but some would give them no guidance when it comes to ethics, morality and values." And columnist William Rassberry added, "In our zeal to get religion out of the classroom, we threw out morality as well."

Mr. Green's radio talk show on CFRA Ottawa, which broadcasts nationally in Canada, took a poll that found that 17 out of 20 families surveyed considered the family not responsible for the action of their children. This means that only 15% of the families in Canada are willing to shoulder their responsibility toward bringing up their children.

Therefore, as parents be aware of this environment. Your children live and interact with the whole of society in schools, shopping centers, that is, wherever they go. Your first step, as a helpful and responsible parent, is recognizing the environment they live in, understanding its impact on their behavior, and then effectively counteracting its influence.

CHAPTER 1

THE OBJECTIVE OF *TARBIYAH*

No doubt, all parents would like to see their children achieve success and happiness in their lives. Similarly, all sincere Muslim parents would like to see themselves and their children admitted to paradise in the hereafter. One gains no benefit in achieving success in this life and loss in the hereafter. Indeed, the correct Islamic *tarbiyah* obtains felicity in this life and in the hereafter.

The objective of *tarbiyah* is to raise children with values and means that will help them to be *righteous* and *happy*. What do we mean by righteous and happy?

Righteousness encompasses all great and good values. It is the embodiment of exalted moral and ethical principles, and manifests as a balanced and moderate life, reflecting positively on the individual's behavior.

Happiness, real happiness, stems from within and results from strong faith and knowledge of the purpose of existence. It is knowledge of the reality of this life, and its true value compared to the hereafter. Man's happiness comes from clearly perceiving life's meaning and understanding the human being's true mission in this life in general and his mission as a Muslim in particular.

During the process of *tarbiyah,* these two qualities cannot be separated. The righteousness of the child will be the cause for his or her continuous happiness in this life and the hereafter. At the same time, a person's happiness demonstrates that he or she understands Islam properly, thus guaranteeing the joy of a wholesome and fruitful life. It guarantees peace of mind, body, and soul. Allah says in the *Qur'an*:

مَنْ عَمِلَ صَالِحًا مِـنْ ذَكَرٍ أَوْ أُنْثَى وَهُـوَ مُؤْمِـنٌ فَلَنُحْيِيَنَّـهُ حَيَـاةً طَيِّـبَةً
وَلَنَجْزِيَنَّهُمْ أَجْرَهُمْ بِأَحْسَنِ مَا كَانُوا يَعْمَلُونَ

Whoever works righteousness, man or woman, and has faith,
verily, to him we will give a life that is good and pure, and
We will bestow on such their reward according to the best of
their actions. (16:97)

Besides needing this generation to be righteous and happy, we
need it to do what we could not do. It is not enough for them to
be a carbon copy of their parents. The challenges they are facing
require qualities that will enable them not only to survive, but to be
real ambassadors of Islam in the West. Among these qualities are
the following:

- STRENGTH IN BELIEF: Even when challenged, they do not change
  their minds just to fit in with the crowd.
- PRIDE IN BEING A MUSLIM: They do not hide the characteristics that
  identify them as Muslims and cause them to be different from those
  around them; in addition, they enjoy telling people about Islam, and
  are good examples of what a Muslim should be.
- CAPABLE AND SKILLFULL: They are able to learn new things with
  relative ease; they utilize information in order to achieve the best and
  most efficient results.
- MOTIVATED: They seek out information and anything else which
  is needed at every opportunity; whenever possible, they help out in
  various worthwhile causes.
- STRONG PERSONALITY: They always present their personal opinions
  and often try to convince people of their point of view; they do not
  change their minds easily, and they enjoy taking on leadership
  positions.
- SELF-CONFIDENT: They don't feel that they must act like their peers;
  they don't let comments about their personalities affect them; and
  they don't always try to prove themselves to other people.
- PROGRESSIVE AND SELF-INITIATING: They motivate other people to
  join good causes because they always take the hardest step; they are
  the first to take causes to higher levels because they are always looking to the ultimate goal—they have the bigger picture in mind.

- SOLUTION-ORIENTED: They don't stop working until they reach the desired result; they don't take personally the problems they might run into along the way; and they make sure the obstacles along the way don't become uncontrollable, keeping the final vision in mind.
- RESOLUTE: They are willing to take risks and enjoy taking on challenges; they don't get discouraged because of obstacles.
- PERSISTENT: The bigger the challenge, the harder they work; they are very patient and persevering, usually exceling at their work.

These qualities can't be acquired without hard work on the part of you, the parents. Starting with honest and sincere soul searching, make sure that what you say and do has the proper impact on your children, that is, supports and motivates them. Parents have to work to create in their child a balanced and strong personality, a positive outlook on life, and confidence that what he or she does will have a positive impact. Not only can parents take what is good and leave what is bad, but they can influence society. They can move it in the right direction by ensuring the exercise of proper moral values for their own well-being and the well-being of generations to come. Below are the six elements of your soul searching process:

Search,
Evaluate,
Acknowledge,
Reinforce,
Change, and
Hang on.

SEARCH within yourself, check your behavior vis-à-vis your children. Dig deep into your childhood and try to find the hidden source of your parental behavior. *Parents Questionnaire #1* will be of great help (see below).

EVALUATE your actions and sayings in your dealings with your children. Which of them are positive, supportive, and based on Islamic values and teachings and which are negative, nonsupportive, and have no basis in Islam. *Parents Questionnaire #2* is an additional aid in your process of self-evaluation (see below).

Parents Questionnaire #1

Answer the following questions as best as you can and be honest with yourself.

During my childhood and teen years:

1. a. I felt my parents loved me because they told me verbally and through hugs and kisses.
   b. My parents neither said they loved me nor did they hug and kiss me, but I could feel their love indirectly at times.
   c. I didn't feel my parents' love and doubted that they loved me at all.

2. a. I felt that my parents were interested and took my personal affairs seriously despite their busy schedules.
   b. I felt that my parents did not pay much attention to my personal affairs and often felt more like one in the crowd.
   c. I didn't get any attention whatsoever from my parents.

3. a. I felt my parents' encouragement and support and they helped me whenever they could.
   b. I didn't feel my parents' encouragement and support and they didn't help me whenever they could.

4. a. I felt my parents' approval and knew that they seriously considered my efforts, no matter what the result was.
   b. I didn't feel my parents' approval except if I took on more than I could to meet their expectations.
   c. I didn't feel my parents' approval no matter what I did.

5. a. My parents were strict with me and expected me to take on responsibilities.
   b. My parents weren't always strict with me and didn't always expect me to take on responsibilities.
   c. My parents were never strict with me and didn't expect me to do anything.

6. a. My parents often compared me with my siblings or other kids we knew which made me very sad.
   b. My parents appreciated me as I was.

7. Write the name of someone who had a positive effect on you during your childhood and growing years.

8. Write the name of someone who had a negative effect on you during your childhood and growing years.

9. Is this person one of your parents?

Parents Questionnaire #2

Please answer the following questions with "yes" or "no."

As a parent:

1. I feel that I had little experience with my first child which caused me to be too strict with him/her.

2. I expect perfection of myself when with my children and often feel like a failure if I haven't been able to do the perfect thing.

3. I feel that cleaning the house and preparing food is more important to me than playing with my children or taking them to the park.

4. I often don't let my children try certain things because I feel that they're difficult and I wasn't able to do them myself when I was a child.

5. I feel that I'm raising my children the same way my parents raised me, despite the difference in time and place. This is because I don't know a better way to raise them.

6. The way I treat my children shows that I don't have confidence in their ability to do things.

7. I let my children decide about simple decisions that are specific to them and reasonable for their age.

8. I feel that the stress and new responsibilities in changing lifestyles are a heavy burden on me and my spouse which doesn't leave enough time or chance for us to deal with all the needs and wants of the children.

ACKNOWLEDGE your findings after you answer the above questions and sort out the positive and negative responses. Again, the positive ones are those which agree with Islamic teachings and suit the environment. The negative ones are those which are mainly from inherited tradition and neither have a basis in Islamic teachings nor suit the environment. Acknowledging your strengths and weaknesses is the first step in improving your parental behavior. Now what you have to do is put your trust in Allah and make a commitment for positive change. Changing unhealthy habits is the key for success as the great scholar Ibn al Qayyim said: "And the core of the matter is in leaving out unhealthy inherited habits."

REINFORCE the positive parental behavior and keep practicing them with your children. If they work, keep using them.

CHANGE the negative parental behavior into positive parental behavior. Work hard on this because change doesn't come easy. It takes hard work to replace bad habits with positive ones. The expected benefits on your childrens' development is too important for you not to try hard enough to change these habits.

HANG ON, don't give up easily. Put your trust in Allah. Keep on trying. Learn new ways and improve your old ways. Positive results are certain if you follow the above steps. It may take a little longer than you think, so don't give up because the reward is so great for those parents who do their best to raise their children.

Here are some of the Prophet Muhammad's sayings on this matter:

When the son of Adam dies, all his or her deeds are cut off except three. These are: continuous charity, useful knowledge that benefits others, and a righteous child who prays for him or her. (Muslim)

Whoever has three daughters, or three sisters, or two daughters, or two sisters and provided them with good company and is pious in dealing with them, this will be his or her pass to paradise. (Tirmidhi and Abu Dawud)

Whoever supports two girls till they attain maturity, he and I will come on the Resurrection Day like this. [And he paired his fingers.] (Muslim)

He also said: "Whoever experienced bringing up daughters, and he treated them well, it will be a protection for him from Hell-Fire." (Agreed upon)

Also in *Surat Yasīn,* verse 12:

$$\text{إِنَّا نَحْنُ نُحْيِ الْمَوْتَى وَنَكْتُبُ مَا قَدَّمُوا وَآثَارَهُمْ وَكُلَّ شَيْءٍ أَحْصَيْنَاهُ}$$

$$\text{فِي إِمَامٍ مُبِينٍ}$$

Verily, We shall give life to the dead, and We record that which they send before and that which they leave behind, and of all things have We taken account in a clear book.

Interpreters agree that "what they leave behind" (*ātharahum*) indicates their offspring and how they were brought up. As such, parents will be greatly rewarded for the effort they make in raising their children in the right way. So work hard. It is worth the effort.

Through the above self/soul searching, parents can learn about themselves and the reason why they behave as they do with their children. For additional help, we list below the major sources of negative parental behavior:

- LACK OF EXPERIENCE: This usually happens with the first child in the family. Both parents have never been through this experience before and don't know what to do. They may have learned some theory, but it is not enough—they need practical experience. Usually asking other parents helps. But one has to be careful not to ask *any* parent. Always try to find someone with a positive and successful experience.

- USING INHERITED METHODS FOR *TARBIYAH*: When we were young, we learned habits and ways of doing things through our parents. These ways may have been suitable for our times and environment, but they are not necessarily suitable for our children and their environment. As parents we can't use the inherited ways and apply them to our children without ensuring that they fit.

- BLIND IMITATION OF OTHERS: Some parents follow others without checking the validity of their *tarbiyah* techniques. This is blind imitation and usually is not healthy. Children are different and what agrees with one child in a certain place may not agree with another in a different place. As parents we always have to try to find what is the best way to deal with our children.

- FULFILLING UNFULFILLED DESIRES THROUGH CHILDREN: Some parents who couldn't achieve their goals during their youth tend to push their children into achieving them. A father who was hoping to be an engineer and couldn't, for one reason or another, may force his son to study engineering. A mother who always wanted to be a medical doctor and couldn't, may push her daughter to study medicine, even if it is not the daughter's desire. This is a major source of negative parental behavior. However, if parents can convince their children that a particular field of study is good for them, that is all right. It is very wrong to push or force children to choose certain areas of study just because the parents like them. Parents should not view their children as extensions of themselves. They are complete human beings who have their own personalities and ambitions.

- DAY-TO-DAY PRESSURES AND LACK OF SKILLS: No doubt, Muslim families living in North America face tremendous day-to-day pressures, especially in their early years of settling in here. These pressures often cause homesickness, especially among women—nonworking mothers—who spend most of their day at home without much involvement in community affairs. Fathers who face the pressure of work outside the home, usually don't want to go out once they return home. They feel tired after a long work day and if the spouses ask them to go out with them they usually prefer to stay home. This is one of the sources of friction between parents and affects their dealings with their children.

The above problem is often easily solved if the housewife acquires a skill like driving. During the day she can visit other Muslim families, socialize with them, and give her children the chance to meet other children of their age. However, Muslim sisters are often handicapped by the traditions of their country of origin which don't allow them to gain practical skills needed for survival in the West. Continuous day-to-day pressures leave parents with the feeling that their children are more of a burden than a blessing and, in this so-called modern society far away from the support of the extended family, are just too difficult to handle.

Boosting your child's self-worth is a very important objective of *tarbiyah*. It is achieved through awareness of how you discourage your child and then avoiding that behavior. Here are three ways:

1.   PERFECTIONISM

It is reported that the Prophet said:

The hasty one neither covers the desired distance nor spares the back of his means of transportation. (Albazzar)

The scholars explain that the "hasty one" is the one who lost the companionship of his fellow travellers because he caused his mount to become fatigued. The perfectionist is similar to the hasty one: he or she asks others to do more than what they can bear, and in the process he causes them to be fatigued. This is not healthy behavior, especially when dealing with children.

Here are two examples of parental perfectionism manifesting on children:

- When Hoda showed Dad her seven "A"s and one "B" report card, he said, "I know you can do better than a 'B,' Hoda, I want to see all 'A's next time." He then laid the report card down with no comment on the higher marks.
- Ali's grandfather sent him a gift on the occasion of *'Id,* so he used his father's computer and produced a thank you note. When it was finished, he showed it to his mother. "This is okay, but the last paragraph is crooked, Ali," she said. "Do it over."

Here we see that perfectionist parents tear down their children's self-esteem by never being satisfied with their accomplishments. Yes, it is good to fine tune some of the children's actions and it is desirable when parents are sure the child's self-esteem can handle it. However, it is important that childrens' efforts be applauded.

Here is what Hoda's dad should have said, "I'm so proud of you, *masha'a Allah,* seven 'A's, dear. I'm sure you must be as happy about this result as I am. You see, Allah always rewards those who work hard and those who try to perfect their work. Allah blessed your efforts and you got these great marks. Congratulations honey." Later Hoda's father could discuss with her in a gentle way what could be done to improve that "B".

Ali's mom too could have encouraged him by saying, "A thank you note for Grandpa? How thoughtful of you. I'm sure it will make him very happy."

Without such comments Hoda and Ali may think nothing they do is acceptable and that will have a negative impact on their self-esteem. Parents should be very careful about being perfectionists.

2.   OVERPROTECTION

Here are two examples of overprotection by parents toward their children:

- Ahmed is 5 years old. He wants to take skating lessons with his friends, but his father says, "That's too dangerous, you remember what happened to my knee when I tried to skate. Maybe you should wait until you become a little bit older."
- Two Muslim families ask Noha to baby-sit, but her mom says no: "Caring for younger children is a big responsibility, Noha. What if something happens to them?"

Here we see that in their attempts to protect Ahmed and Noha, the parents cross the thin line between protection and discouragement. The father uses his bad experience as an excuse to deprive Ahmed of skating lessons. Yes, caution is necessary sometimes, depending on the circumstances, but children may believe that Mom or Dad think they are stupid or incapable. In the case of Noha, her parents should have given her the chance and equiped her with the proper precautions, such as checking on her every hour by phone and preparing a contact list for emergencies.

Parents should remember that bruised knees will heal, but low self-esteem can last a lifetime.

3.   HUMILIATION

When Allah tells us:

$$\text{يَـٰٓأَيُّهَا ٱلَّذِينَ آمَنُوا . . . وَ لَا تَنَابَزُوا بالالْقَابِ}$$

O you who believe . . . do not humiliate one another by calling each other (offensive) nicknames . . . (49:11)

This applies to everyone. Even more so when we deal with our children. Humiliation destroys a child's self-esteem. Here are two examples of parents humiliating their children:

- Fatima, a fifth grader, cannot watch TV until her homework is finished. She knew that part of her project was due the next day, but she wanted to watch her favorite figure skating show. So she lied to her mother. The next day her teacher called to ask about the assignment, and Fatima's mother was furious. She stormed to the driveway where Fatima was skipping rope with her friends. "Fatima, you are such a liar!" she yelled, "You ought to be ashamed of yourself!" Fatima wanted to crawl under a rock as her buddies snickered.
- Faisal gained weight between third and fourth grade, and his mother started calling him "Chub." " Faisal, you need to stop eating so much so you can be slim like other boys," said his mom. "Your brother is older than you and he doesn't weigh as much as you do." Faisal hung his head and cried.

The mothers of Fatima and Faisal thought they were motivating and correcting their children, but they were really humiliating them. Humiliation is a common way to rob a child of self-esteem.

Every mom and dad has a parenting style based on his or her personality type, background, and experience. Experts say that there are four. They are the following:

Permissive
Free-reigning
Authoritarian, and
Controlling

These styles have strengths and weaknesses, but in general, they either build self-esteem or tear it down. The fifth style is the ideal one: nurturing and setting limits.

If your style becomes extreme, your child's self-esteem may possibly be scarred. Although most parents fall somewhere between overly permissive and controlling, you should know the strengths and weaknesses of your style as a parent and make adjustments that move you toward the ideal. Let us now provide some details about these styles so you can discover which style best describes you.

1. PERMISSIVE. A permissive father often has trouble setting boundaries. He will make comments like this, "All right, you can stay up A'isha, I know you like this program." Or he will say, "Didn't you hear me calling you for dinner? Well, sit down, I'll put your plate in the microwave so you won't have to eat cold food." You see, this father is a strong nurturer and a weak limit-setter.

2. FREE-REIGNING. A free-reigning mother will sometimes get too wrapped up in her own affairs to tend adequately to the needs of her son. She'll say, "Ahmed, if you think I'm stupid, that's your problem." Or, "Work it out yourself. I'm busy." This type of mother is weak in nurturing and in limit-setting.

3. AUTHORITARIAN. An authoritarian father will often fail to listen to his daughter or show respect for her ideas or opinions. He makes comments like, "It's time for bed, and no arguments Fatima." Or, "You are late for supper, that means you don't eat tonight." This father is a weak nurturer and strong limit-setter.

4. CONTROLLING. Controlling parents nurture and set limits for their children, but frequently go overboard in supervising them, a trait common among perfectionistic parents. A mother of this type will make a comment like, "Asmā', get off the floor or you'll get your clothes dirty." Or, "Ali, this is what I want you to wear to the mosque." This type of a mother is a strong nurturer, but she sets too many limits.

5. THE RIGHT BALANCE BETWEEN NURTURING AND SETTING LIMITS. Moderation is promoted by Islam in every aspect of life. Allah says in the *Qur'an*:

$$وَكَذَلِكَ جَعَلْنَاكُمْ أُمَّةً وَسَطًا$$

And thus we have made you an ummah of moderation (justly balanced). (2:143)

On this basis the ideal parents are those who achieve the right balance between nurturing and limit-setting. They are firm in setting limits, yet they allow children freedom within those limits. They make comments like, "Sumaiya, I wish I could let you stay up, but there is school tomorrow, and I don't feel good about you missing out on the sleep you need." Or, "You are late again for dinner Ali. How can we work this out?" This illustrates the ideal balance between encouraging children and disciplining them.

Most parents see themselves in one or more of the above categories. Your goal is to build your strengths, work on your weaknesses and try to move toward the ideal. Here are some suggestions to help you begin this move:

- *Be honest with yourself.* Circle the quotes from the above examples that sound most like you. Find out with which parenting style you identify with, and into which category you fall.

- *Encourage yourself.* Make a list of your parenting strengths and how they can benefit your children.

- *Encourage your children.* Note one weakness in your parenting style. What message does it send to your children? What can you do this week to make this message more encouraging? Can you say to them I'm sorry for this and adjust your style to improve this weakness.

- *Talk to knowledgeable members in your community,* especially those who have some religious knowledge and practical experience in successfully raising good, well-behaved, and confident children. Have regular meetings with them and learn from their experiences.

- *Make a decision.* No matter what style characterizes you, decide and promise yourself not to overprotect, humiliate, or demand perfection from your children. After all Allah says:

$$\text{لَا يُكَلِّفُ اللَّهُ نَفْسًا إِلَّا وُسْعَهَا}$$

Allah does not put a burden on any soul more than what it can bear. (2:286)

The Prophet said:

Whatever I order you, do as much as you can. (Agreed upon)

- *Use this book.* Use various principles and experiences detailed in this book to modify and improve your style. It is the purpose of this book to help you raise happy and righteous children with high self-esteem.

To help you realize all of the above, the next chapter will discuss the basic principles of *tarbiyah* gleaned from the *Qur'an* and the practices of our blessed Prophet Muhammad.

Before we start a new section, a few important points have to be emphasized:

1. Parents should always make it clear to their children that the source of all that they say to them and all that they ask them to do are acts of training, as ordained by Allah and His messenger. In this way, the children will feel they are not only interacting with their parents but with something greater than them, Allah and His Messenger. They know that when they obey their dedicated and committed Muslim parents they are actually obeying a higher authority, that is, Allah and the Prophet Muhammad.

2. Raising children is the noblest role. Parents should feel the truth of this. They are preparing the next generation to fulfill the real purpose of human existence on earth. Indeed, they should feel that the baby in their arms is a person who will bear responsibilities and make serious decisions which may affect all Muslims and maybe all of humanity.

3. Parents should realize that they not only have to teach their children what is right and what is wrong, but also they have to provide them with the tools—the criteria—to make appropriate decisions in any given environment—including a possible hostile environment here in North America. As a parent, you will not always be with your children. Thus, it is important that from an early age they be trained to use their knowledge to make decisions on their own in a variety of situations.

4. The objective is to raise children who are confident with high self-esteem, who firmly believe in what they say and what they do. This confidence and self-respect should be balanced.

It should be based on the ability of the children to develop and utilize the potentials given to them by Allah. It should never be based on belittling other children, ridiculing, or looking down upon them.

5.   As parents, you want to raise children who are flexible, open minded, and fair. They need to consider that other children have similar rights and duties.

6.   Instructing children without serving as role models, parents do not serve the *tarbiyah* process. Children do what they see. You are what you do, not what you say. Brains remember actions and memories register pictures. More on this subject in the section on "Ways and Means of *Tarbiyah.*"

Summary

In this chapter, we discussed the main objectives of Islamic *Tarbiyah* and indicated that these objectives are to raise children who are righteous, happy and have high self-confidence. The qualities needed for our children to successfully face the challenges ahead of them were briefly discussed. We suggested to parents to engage in a self-searching process to identify the sources of negative parental behaviour they may have and replace them with positive ones. We provided two questionnaires and a list of the sources of negative parental behaviour to help guide the parents in this process. Examples on how parents can discourage their children and cause them to have low self-esteem by exercising perfectionism, overprotection, and humiliation were presented. Various parenting styles were also discussed. These are, permissive, free-reigning, authoritarian, and controlling. We concluded with the recommendation that the best parenting style is achieved through following the moderate way, where parents establish the right balance between nurturing and setting limits.

CHAPTER 2

BASIC PRINCIPLES OF *TARBIYAH*
FROM THE *QUR'AN* AND *SUNNAH*

The basic principles of *tarbiyah* are laid out in the *Qur'an* and teachings of the Prophet Muhammad. During the course of our research, in which we came across many useful books written by Muslim and non-Muslim authors, we found that most good principles find substantiation in an *ayat* of the *Qur'an* or in a tradition from the Prophet. The *Qur'an* and *Sunnah* are the best sources for providing a framework and guidelines for children's upbringing.

Let us now explore some of these basic principles and see how they can help us in the noble task at hand.

UNDERSTAND YOUR CHILD

In order to know how to motivate children to function in a useful and cooperative way, we must have some understanding of the psychological mechanism involved.

All human actions are driven by a purpose—either known or unknown to the person. This applies to both adults and children. As a parent, knowing this hidden purpose will enable you to help your child behave differently by changing the motives. A child has two major motives that drive his or her actions—the need to belong and the need to gain attention.

The need to belong is a child's basic need, as it is, later, for adults too. A child feels secure when he or she has his or her place in the group—at home within the family, and at school within the classroom. From infancy, children explore ways of finding their place in the family. Unconsciously, they repeat actions that bring them attention and abandon actions that make them feel left out.

People feel they belong to a certain community or group if they have something in common with the other members. Common activities create bonds between those who share them. For children to satisfy such needs in the school environment, they have to take part in some of the interactions/activities going on with their peers. This participation ensures that they have something in common with classmates. A common mistake that some parents fall into is not giving their children permission to be part of any extra curricular school activities. This decision deprives children from satisfying the need to belong while in school. A better way of dealing with such situations is for parents to help their children identify activities that don't conform to Islamic etiquette and therefore, should be avoided. Meanwhile, they should also help their children select "neutral" school activities to participate in.

Another way to help your children satisfy this need is to allow them to watch sports, such as hockey, figure skating or basketball on TV so they have something to talk about with other children in school.

In addition, children need to feel that they are being noticed, as they are anxious for attention. If a child is playing nicely, unnoticed, he or she will try to attract attention through fights and mischief in order to be noticed. A child would rather be noticed as a bad child than ignored as a well-behaved one.

Children are expert observers, but they make many mistakes in interpreting what they observe. For example, when there is a newborn child in the family, an older child may resort to immature behavior because of the attention given to the newborn. The parents can correct this behavior by allowing the older child to get the parents' attention. They can involve the older child in helping out with the new baby's care and praising him or her for the help. A child notices all the attention given to the baby, but draws wrong conclusions and chooses mistaken ways to find his or her place either within the family, or society.

It is also important to understand how a child reacts when faced with an obstacle, whether it is a physical handicap, a learning disability, or moving to a new and unfamiliar environment. Children with courage gained from positive and supportive training work hard to overcome obstacles. Children who lack courage give up. Either they do not mix with others or they follow the crowd in everything they do, whether right or wrong.

KEY FACTORS AFFECTING CHILD'S PERSONALITY

The following three key factors affect a child's personality: family atmosphere, position within the family, and training methods. They are detailed below.

1.   FAMILY ATMOSPHERE

The family is the child's first environment and has a great impact on his personality. The relationship between the parents sets up the pattern for all other relationships in the family. If the parents are respectful, loving, and merciful to each other, if they tolerate each other, if they show care and gentleness toward each other, the child's personality will reflect these beautiful qualities that are common to all the family members.

Negative Family Atmosphere

Disciplining children is a shared responsibility. The father should not undermine the mother's orders related to discipline without first discussing the matter with her privately. This should never be done in front of the children. Spouses should not overburden themselves with more than what they can deal with.

In some cases, the father may do nothing to bring up the children; he may even hinder their training by undermining the mother's orders in front of the children. On the other hand, the mother may do nothing useful for her children all day long and when the children do something she tells them to wait till their father comes back. Both attitudes are wrong. Both parents should have a clear *tarbiyah* plan which is studied and mutually agreed upon. *Tarbiyah* requires planning. Parents should lead the *tarbiyah* train and not be left to react time after time to the behavior of their children.

The attitude of the family toward spending money, achievement and effort, success and contribution, and other races and differences are all observed and absorbed by the children.

Dealing fairly with all your children, not favoring one of them over another, contributes positively to your children's personality and is important to a healthy family atmosphere.

Cooperation between parents and family members is another positive quality in helping the child develop a good personality. Moderation in everything enhances a balanced personality.

Healthy and Positive Family Atmosphere

The significance of early religious training is well-recognized. Practicing Islam in front of the children and providing an Islamic atmosphere in the home is very important in linking the child with Allah.

Children experience society through the relationship between their parents. In every family, children will have certain common characteristics; they are the expression of the family atmosphere. However, all children in a family are not alike.

2. A CHILD'S POSITION WITHIN THE FAMILY

The dynamics associated with a child's position within the family is another important factor that influences his personality. As we indicated before, a child is continuously searching to find his or her place in the family. For example, in a family composed of a husband, wife, and one child, the child is always receiving and enjoying attention from his or her parents. He or she is the only child, the first child, and all the family time is for him alone. He or she interacts mainly with two adults—receiving more than giving. When a second child arrives, it represents a threat to the first child. The dynamics are now different for the first child. The new comer now receives more attention, but unlike the older child he or she already has an older brother or sister. The older child is now observing all the attention given to the baby and based on the family atmosphere, interprets this attention in his or her own way.

Competition for the attention of parents begins, and the first child has to find his or her new position within the family. If the family atmosphere is encouraging, the child adjusts and establishes a new position in which he or she is helpful and contributes more than the baby. At this point, if the older child gets discouraged, he or she may resort to misbehaving and finds his or her position as the bad one in the family, as long as it gets him or her the attention he or she needs.

With the birth of every consecutive child, the family dynamics change and each child has to reestablish his or her position. One child may choose to be the achiever, while another may select to be the helpless one. A third may go for the pleasing personality, the helping one, or the child may have to choose to be the bad one. The position a child takes at this point may leave a life long impression.

Cooperation between the parents is essential to ensure that every child finds his or her place within the family peacefully. When parents know the importance of working together, they can help their children find their position in the family by giving them the opportunity of being useful.

3. Genetic Dispositions

These are the tendencies that Allah SWT puts in every human being. The Qur'an hints at these tendencies in chapter 91 verses 7 & 8 when Allah (SWT) says what can be translated to: "And [by] the soul and He who proportioned it. And inspired it [with discernment of] its wickedness and its righteousness." This means that humans have the tendency to do bad things as well as to do good things. It means that humans have the tendency to acquire good qualities and habits as well as bad ones. This is as far as nature can go; just instilling various tendencies and inclinations in us. As such, no individual is forced to be bad or is condemned to be bad and wicked by nature. The Qur'an continues in the next two verses of the same chapter to emphasize this fact. It says what can be translated as: "He has succeeded who purifies it. And he has failed who instills it [with corruption]." This shows us that nobody is naturally bad and nobody is naturally good. Rather, every person has tendencies of goodness and wickedness. Those who want to be good nurture the tendencies of goodness and those who turn out to be bad and wicked usually nurture the tendencies of wickedness.

Let us now project the above concept on children and the world of parenting to understand parents' roles in helping their child develop a balanced and positive personality. In the early years of children's lives, we may notice that some children are more aggressive than others, and some are more forward and outgoing while others are quiet and more on the shy side. Parents may also witness a child who easily remembers words and seems to enjoy any exercise of memorization, be it Qur'an memorization or songs and anasheed. On the other hand, the same parent may witness his or her other child resisting memorization and trying any and every thing to avoid such an exercise. These are all indications of the natural tendencies each child has.

As parents, our role is to recognize our children's inherent tendencies and use various positive parenting methods to make sure that our children grow up to be well-rounded and balanced Muslims. Allah (SWT) emphasizes the importance of balance and moderation in all things when He (SWT) says in chapter 2 verse 143 what could be translated to: "And thus We have made you a median (Justly balanced) *Ummah.*"

We shouldn't just leave our children to live in their comfort zone and act according to what comes naturally to them. For example, if a parent notices that his child is naturally shy and would rather play alone than in a group all the time, the parent should take steps to help this child develop a more balanced personality. For instance, the parent could invite a playmate over for his shy son or daughter and encourage them to play cooperatively together so the child learns how to interact with others and breaks out of his or her comfort zone. The parent could also take his shy son or daughter to the park and, instead of allowing the child to sit by his side and watch the other kids play, the parent could get the child involved with other kids so that the shy child can learn some new social skills. Likewise, if a parent notices that her child is temperamental by nature and gets angry easily, steps need to be taken to modify this behaviour so it is more balanced.

4. TRAINING METHODS

The training method is the fourth factor that affects a child's personality. The rest of this chapter and the chapter "Ways and Means of *Tarbiyah*" are dedicated to this subject. The training methods that a child is subjected to have a great impact on his or her personality. If the methods used are tough and imbalanced, the child's personality will be immoderate and may select extreme views in his adult life. If the methods are not accompanied by practical examples, the child will differentiate between words and actions and will not take future instructions seriously. So be careful of what you do with your children. To understand the influence of your methods on your children's personalities, let us now discuss more basic principles of *tarbiyah*.

LINK THE CHILD TO ALLAH

Linking the child to Allah is a very important and continuous process for Muslims. It starts at birth. The Prophet has instructed us to say the *adhān* (the call to prayer) in a newborn's right ear and the *iqamah* (the second call to prayer) in its left ear immediately after birth. Thus, the first words the child hears are the call to prayer. From then on, ensure that your child is hearing the name of Allah, the recitation of the *Qur'an*, *tasbīh* (repetitive mentioning of God and his attitributes), and *du'a* (supplication), even though he or she is very young and doesn't understand the meanings. Take your child with you when you make your *jumu'ah* prayers, and carry him or her after the prayer while doing the *tasbih* or even do the *tasbih* on the child's hand.

Parents, it is important to present Allah to your child as positive, protective, and loving, and not as threatening and frightening. Unfortunately, when some parents present Allah to their children, they paint, by what they say and how they say it, a picture of Allah as a punishing God. For example, a mother tells her child, "If you don't do such and such a thing, Allah will put you in the hellfire."

Not only this, some parents repeat the same threat to their children over and over again. This is wrong and paints the wrong picture of Allah. Young children get frightened easily. Talk to them about Allah positively. For example, say, "Allah loves you because you helped your sister." Or, "Allah loves you because you perform your prayers."

You can create situations that make your children feel that Allah is helping them. One way of doing this is when children misplace something. Help the child to find it while they are making the prayer for lost items:

> O Allah, O He who guides to whatever has been lost, guide me to what I am looking for!

When they find it, they will feel that Allah has helped them.

Ensure that your children understand that authority belongs to Allah, and that even you, their parents, are subject to His authority. To achieve this, give practical examples and practice what you preach. In front of the children, perform your prayers, fast, and tell the truth.

Create situations in which your children can witness that others are also subject to Allah's authority and that they must also pray, fast, and tell the truth. Achieve this by visiting other Muslim families and participating in mosque activities and Islamic events.

Have mercy, do your best, and pray to Allah for best results.

MERCY

Mercy is the essence of Islam. In the Qur'an, Allah tells His messenger:

$$\text{وَمَا أَرْسَلْنَاكَ إِلا رَحْمَةً لِلْعَالَمِينَ}$$

We have not sent you, but as a *mercy* to all creatures. (21:107)

In another verse, He tells Muhammad:

$$\text{وَلَوْ كُنْتَ فَظًّا غَلِيظَ الْقَلْبِ لانْفَضُّوا مِنْ حَوْلِكَ}$$

Had you been stern and harsh hearted, they would have dispersed from around you. (3:159)

It is narrated that a beduin saw the Prophet kissing his grandson, and said, "I have ten children, yet I have never kissed anyone of them." The Prophet said, "We have nothing to do with those harsh-hearted people. A person who shows no mercy to others, Allah will show no mercy to him."

Parents, deal with each other and your children in a way that reflects Allah's mercy. This does not mean that you should not be firm with the children. Maintain both mercy and firmness while performing *tarbiyah*. Later, we will give some examples. Children should see and feel a merciful relationship between their parents. They should feel it in the way their parents treat each other, and in the way they help each other. They should not detect the least trace of harshness in their parents' relationship. Husbands should help their wives in various things related to the house, especially in things related to the children's *tarbiyah*. The Prophet Muhammad was seen helping his family in their household chores. It is reported that he told his companions:

The best of you is the one who is best with his family and among you I am the best to my family.

Unfortunately, it is quite customary among some Eastern husbands to leave all children's matters to the mothers. Many husbands tell their wives, "Children are your responsibility." This is not the right attitude. On the other hand, some wives may neglect their children's needs all day, waiting for their husbands to return from work. This attitude is uncooperative and does not reflect any mercy. Children's upbringing is a responsibility to be shared by both husband and wife, performed in a well-planned and studied manner. Relationships based on mercy among members of the family create a very positive and conducive environment, fostering *tarbiyah.*

Here are some more examples that illustrate the Prophet's mercy toward children:

- Those who have a child should act like a child with him.
- He used to line up Abdullah, Ubaydullah and Kuthayr, the sons of his Uncle Abbas and ask them to run toward him, saying, "Whoever wins the race I'll give him so and so." They used to come running, jump to hug him and he would kiss them.
- Abu Hurayrah said that the Prophet took Hasan's hand and put his feet on his own feet and told him, "Climb up."
- Jaber narrates that he saw the Prophet crawling on his hands and knees while Hasan and Husayn were riding on his back. He said, "The best riders are you and the best camel is yours."
- It is reported by Anas that he said, "I have never seen anybody more merciful to children than the Prophet."
- Anas also reported that whenever the Prophet passed children on the road, he would give them a smile and a greeting.
- "He is not considered from us who does not have mercy for our young and respect for our old."

GENTLENESS, KINDNESS, LENIENCY AND LOVE

'A'ishah (beloved wife of the Prophet) reported that the Messenger of Allah said, "Allah is kind and He loves kindness in all affairs" (agreed upon).

She also reported that the Messenger of Allah said, "Allah is kind and He loves kindness and confers upon kindness that which He does not confer upon severity or anything else besides it." (Muslim)

Again on the authority of 'A'ishah, the Messenger of Allah is reported to have said, "Kindness is not found in anything but adds beauty to it, and if it is withdrawn from anything it defects it. (Muslim)

Jarīr ibn Abdullah reported that he heard the Messenger of Allah say, "He who is deprived of leniency is deprived of goodness." (Muslim)

Ibn Abbas reported that he heard the Messenger of Allah say to Ashaj Abd al Qays, "You possess two such qualities that Allah loves. These are forbearance and leniency." (Muslim)

Abu Hurayra reported that a bedouin urinated in the mosque and some people rushed to beat him. Whereupon, the Messenger of Allah orderd them not to harm him and to pour a tumbler of water over it to wash it out. Then he said to his companions, "You have been sent to make things easy and not to make them difficult." (Bukhari)

Allah SWT also describes the Prophet pbuh as very kind and merciful to the believers at the end of Surah TAWBAH, "Verily there has come unto you a messenger from among yourselves. It grieves him that you should receive any injury or difficulty. He is anxious over you; for the believers full of pity, kind and merciful" (Q 9, V 128)

These hadiths emphasize the importance of kindness and gentleness in relations with others. They are wonderful qualities for parents to have, greatly enhancing the *tarbiyah* process of their children.

To illustrate the kindness of the Prophet pbuh: even when he gave advice to someone he was very considerate and used the best wording, especially with young people. It was narrated that he, pbuh, told Jaber when he was young, advising him on the proper manners of eating: oh my dear son, mention the name of Allah and eat with your right hand and eat from the closest part of the dish to you. Notice the word used by him "oh my dear son", *Ya-Bonay*, as if the person is his own son. The *Qura'n* also uses the same term for the advice of Luqman to his son, "Behold, Luqman said to his son by way of gentle advice: 'O my dear son, join not in worship others with Allah, for false worship is indeed the highest wrong doing' " (Q 31, V 13).

The Prophet pbuh also used similar term when he was advising Ibn Abbas to adhere to the orders of Allah and safeguard the commandments of Allah and that, as a result Allah will be with him, supporting and protecting him. On that occasion, he was riding behind the prophet pbuh as was reported by At-Tirmizi. At the beginning of his advice, the prophet pbuh used the term *"Ya-Ghulam"* which is a gentle word used to describe preteens and early teenagers.

In all of the above examples, there is a great lesson for parents to follow. It is quite unfortunate that some parents deal with their children in a very harsh way, especially when they make mistakes. Being gentle, kind, and using a merciful but firm voice when instructing your child has at least four benefits. These are:

1. You are rewarded for using the prophet's way of dealing with things

2. It always brings better results, according to the above sayings of the prophet pbuh

3. Your child feels that you love him and you want the best for him, and not just that you're venting your anger

4. It keeps the channel of communication open between you and your child, which is very important for the teen years

TEACH THEM RESPECT

Being kind and merciful towards children does not mean that you should let them behave disrespectfully towards their parents in particular and others in general. The Prophet pbuh said, "He is not from us the one who does not respect our elders and has no mercy for our young ones". The glorious *Qura'n* emphasizes showing respect for both parents in so many places. In *Surah Israa'*, verses 23 and 24 Allah says, "Thy lord has decreed that you worship none but Him, and that you be kind to parents. Whether one or both of them attain old age in their life say not to them a word of contempt, nor repel them but address them in terms of honor. And out of kindness, lower to them the wing of humility, and say: 'My Lord! Bestow on them Your mercy even as they cherished me in childhood.'" (Q 17, V 23-24). Also in *Surah Baqara*, verse 83, Allah says, "And remember We took a covenant from the children of Israel (to this effect): worship none but Allah; treat with kindness your parents and kindred, and orphans and those in need; speak fair to the people; be steadfast in prayer; and give *Zakat...*" (Q 2 -V 83).

Children need to see respect demonstrated to parents and other elders in their everyday lives. North American culture makes it very difficult for children to pick up this quality without genuine effort, consistent guidance and continuous training from parents. In this society, children always hear comments like "why not", "it's not fair", and "I don't care" from their peers as well as from other adults. These types of comments and behaviours don't promote respect. They are based on the North American individualistic attitude. These comments are self-centered and are only concerned with what the speaking individual wants without considering anyone else. Also, it has become very common among children to make faces while they are talking to their parents at home or their teachers at school. This attitude has become such a habit for some children that most of the time they don't even feel that they are making faces. This is another form of disrespect and should not be tolerated.

Parents need to work hard to make sure their children understand what is respectful and what is not. This can be easily done by always treating each other with respect so that the children have a living example who treat the child in a respectful way, and consistently instruct, train and demand of the child to do respectful things.

For example, when they make faces while talking to you, remind them that they are making faces and tell them, "look at me, am I making faces while talking to you? Please don't make faces when you talk to me." Also, teach them to say "please" and "thank you" whenever they ask for something or something is given to them. Even a situation so simple as thanking their mother for the food at the dinner table gives them an idea of how much their parents do for them.

Even when disagreeing, the children should be taught to do it with respect. For instance, say the parents take the children to the park to play. When it is time to go, the children ask, "Can we stay longer?" After the parents explain that it is time to go, the children insist that they still want to play. They begin to say, "It's not fair. Why do we have to go?" The parents should not tolerate this. If the children see that this disrespectful attitude is accepted, they will continue to behave like this. It is all right to let the children ask politely to stay longer, but they should remember to say please and to know where the limit is and when to stop asking.

BREVITY IN PREACHING

Allah the Exalted and Almighty has said:

$$ادْعُ إِلَى سَبِيلِ رَبِّكَ بِالْحِكْمَةِ وَالْمَوْعِظَةِ الْحَسَنَةِ$$

Invite to the way of your Lord with wisdom and kind advice. (16:125)

Using wisdom when inviting others for the path of Allah, or when correcting any negative behaviour of individuals is highly recommended because of its great impact on people's reaction. If this wisdom is coupled with gentle and kind advice, the result is usually positive and people respond favorably to the advice provided. The prophet may Allah's peace and blessings be upon him always observed this principle in molding the personalities of his companions and correcting or rectifying their mistakes. Not only this but he never bored them with repeated instructions at times that may not be suitable, nor he did it in a harsh way. The following two hadeeths clearly illustrates this wonderful behaviour of the prophet:

> Abi Wa'il Shaqiq bin Salama reported that Ibn Mas'ud used to preach every Thursday. A man said to him, "Abu Abd al Rahman, we like your talk, we would like you to lecture to us every day." He replied, "There is nothing to hinder me from preaching and giving you a lecture every day, except that I fear boring you. I follow the same method in preaching to you as the Messenger of Allah adopted in preaching to us, which was that he feared boring us." (Agreed upon)

The Messenger of Allah was very wise and kind in teaching his companions and correcting their mistakes. Mu'awiyah ibn al Hakam al Sulami said,

> While I was in the prayer with the Messenger of Allah, a man in the congregation sneezed and I responded with, "Allah have mercy on you." The people stared at me with disapproving looks. So I said, "Why are you staring at me?" Thereupon they began to strike their hands on their thighs. When I saw them urging me to remain silent, I became angry but restrained myself. When the Messenger of Allah concluded his prayer (I declare that neither before him nor after him have I seen a leader who gave better instruction than him), he neither remonstrated with me, beat me, nor reproved me. He said, "It is not permissible to talk during the prayer because it consists of glorifying Allah, declaring His greatness and recitation of *Qur'an*," or words to that effect. (Muslim)

These examples show very clearly that the prophet pbuh understood the psychological state of mind of human beings and treated his companions accordingly. When you preach excessively, this may have the opposite effect on the individual you are trying to communicate with. Children are no different. If you hammer them with one piece of advice after the other in an intense and excessive way, they will respond negatively and feel that you are picking on them or pushing them to do more than they can.

It is of utmost importance that parents should observe this principle of being wise and kind when they want to direct or correct their children's behaviour. Great many parents nag their children so often and on a regular basis. They boss them around at every opportunity, and instruct them to do various things. Some parents may even order their children in a harsh and unpleasant way to do things that may not be within their capability. Preaching and reminding by parents should be done on an occasional basis and in a gentle and kind way taking into consideration the age of the child, his level of comprehension, and his ability to act. In the case of prayer, which is the most important pure ritual for a Muslim, the prophet may Allah's peace and blessings be upon him instructed us to provide at least three years of training for our children to perform it before inflecting any kind of punishment on them.

Dear parent, please follow the way of the Prophet pbuh, advise them occasionally, and be brief in your exhortation.

NEVER RESORT TO FORCE

Abu Hurayrah reported that the Messenger of Allah said,

The strong person is not the one who wrestles but the strong person is the one who controls himself in a fit of rage. (Agreed upon)

It is reported that 'A'ishah said:

The hand of the Messenger of Allah never hit a servant or a woman, but of course he fought in the cause of Allah. He never took revenge from anyone for the torture inflicted upon him, but of course he exacted retribution for the sake of Allah when the injunctions of Allah were violated. (Muslim)

Abu Mas'ud al Badry reported the following:

I was beating my slave with a whip when I heard a voice behind me saying, "Abu Mas'ud, bear in mind." I didn't recognize the voice due to my anger. As he came near me, I found that it was the Messenger of Allah who was saying, "Abu Mas'ud, bear in mind. Abu Masud, bear in mind." I threw the whip from my hand. The Prophet said, "Bear in mind, Abu Mas'ud. Verily Allah has more dominance over you than you have over your slave." After that, I never beat my servant." (Muslim)

The above hadiths indicate that the Prophet of Allah never used force against children or women, and clearly instructed his companions not to use force against anyone, especially children and women. Parents should always find other disciplinary measures, and never resort to beating or using force with their children. Some of these measures are explained later in this book.

FAVORITISM IS NOT ALLOWED

Al Nu'man ibn Bashir said:

My father conferred upon me a slave as a gift. He took me to Allah's Messenger to get a witness. The Messenger of Allah said, "Have you given a gift to every son of yours such as you have awarded Al Nu'man." He [my father] said, "No." The Messenger of Allah said, "Be mindful of your obligation to Allah and do justice in respect of your children." My father came back and revoked his gift. (Agreed upon)

Al Nu'man has also reported that the Messenger of Allah said, "Treat your children equally, treat your children equally, treat your children equally" (Ahmad, Ibn Haban, and the Sunnan).

It is very clear from this incident and this hadith that parents shouldn't favor one child over another, especially in material matters. This doesn't mean that parents are going to buy exactly the same gift for every child they have, particularly if the children are not within the same age range. It means that they can buy a different gift, but of a similar value, or a gift that is acceptable by the child and suitable for his age group. It is important to note here that fairness is not limited to gifts and material aspects of life only, but it also covers the emotional and psychological feelings of your child. Parents should try their best to equally distribute the time they devote to play with their children and the attention they are giving to each of them, even the hugs and kisses. Here are some practical situations to look out for in avoiding favoritism:

˘ When going out, parents should take turns taking different children out with them.

˘ Parents should make a point of attending their children's school functions or special events, such as school plays and sports tournaments, equally.

˘ Parents should cater the time they spend with each child to the activities and interests of that particular child. Don't assume that because your oldest son likes to play baseball, this is what his younger brother will want to do.

˘ If one of your children requires more help with his school work, don't count this out of the fun time you spend with him.

˘ Don't take sides with your favorite child in the case of a conflict. Always look at the facts and use them as your judge for the situation. Parents who take sides or favor one child over the rest only stir resentment between their children and generate sibling rivalry.

The Prophet pbuh, when he sat in a gathering with his companions, would leave every one of them with the impression that he was the most beloved person to the Prophet pbuh. This is an important lesson for parents to always try their best to leave the same impression with all of their children, even if their love for one child is more than for the rest.

EVERY SOUL IS ACCOUNTABLE FOR WHAT IT EARNS

Allah speaks of accountability in the following ayāt:

كُلُّ نَفْسٍ بِمَا كَسَبَتْ رَهِينَةٌ

Every soul is responsible for what it earns. (74:38)

مَنِ اهْتَدَى فَإِنَّمَا يَهْتَدِي لِنَفْسِهِ وَمَنْ ضَلَّ فَإِنَّمَا يَضِلُّ عَلَيْهَا وَلا تَـزِرُ وَازِرَةٌ وِزْرَ أُخْرَى

Whoever chooses to follow the right path, follows it but for his own good; and whoever goes astray, goes but astray to his own hurt; and no bearer of burdens shall be made to bear another's burden. (17:15)

لا يُكَلِّفُ اللَّهُ نَفْسًا إِلا وُسْعَهَا لَهَا مَا كَسَبَتْ وَعَلَيْهَا مَا اكْتَسَبَتْ

God does not burden any human being with more than he is well able to bear: in his favour shall be whatever good he does, and against him whatever evil he does. (2:286)

فَمَنْ يَعْمَلْ مِثْقَالَ ذَرَّةٍ خَيْرًا يَرَه وَمَنْ يَعْمَلْ مِثْقَالَ ذَرَّةٍ شَرًّا يَرَه

And so, he who shall have done an atom's weight of good, shall behold it; and he who shall have done an atom's weight of evil, shall behold it. (99:7–8)

These verses establish the concept of accountability and represent one of the basic principles in dealing with children. Children should be held accountable for what they do. They should feel the weight of the consequences of their deeds and mistakes. In the absence of accountability and without feeling the burden of consequences of their deeds, the same mistakes will be repeated over and over.

Children will not learn their limits, that is, where to stop, what to do and what not to do. Here is a practical illustration of how parents sometimes fail to apply this principle, possibly giving the wrong message to their children and causing them to continue repeating the wrong/negative behaviour.

"Ahmad is a grade three student. He uses the school bus daily to go to school. The school bus pick-up spot for Ahmad is one block away from his house at 7:45 AM, sharp. More often than not, Ahmad misses the bus because he doesn't like to wait for it and only leaves home in a rush at the last minute. When this happens, Ahmad's Mom usually drives him to school. This type of behaviour from Mom doesn't reinforce positive practices on Ahmad's part. He will continue to behave in the same way, since he hasn't felt the weight of the consequences of his actions."

You may ask, what is the solution in a case like this? The solution lies in Mom making sure that Ahmad feels the consequences of his actions. The approach she uses will depend on Ahmad's personality. If Ahmad is a good student and enjoys going to school, Mom won't drive him to school for one day. Yes, he is going to miss one school day, but he will learn a good accountability lesson through such an action and due to the extra work he will have to do to catch up for what he missed that day. If Ahmad is an average student and staying home may be perceived by him as a reward rather than punishment, Mom should think of another way for him to feel the consequences of his actions. May be she should drive him to school but in the same time deduct from his allowance the equivalence of a bus ticket, or ask him to do some extra house chores to compensate for his mom's wasted time.

Another example is if Ahmad forgets his lunch bag at home almost regularly as he rushes to catch the school bus. If Mom takes the lunch bag and delivers it to his school, Ahmad will not learn any lesson and may continue to repeat the same mistake. If Mom ignores the situation and leaves Ahmad without a lunch, he will learn that there are consequences of his actions.

It is important to note here that parents should only use this principle when the bad behaviour of the child becomes a pattern, i.e. it is being repeated frequently. Parents should avoid using this technique with the first mistake. They should leave some room for accommodation and give their child the chance to correct his mistakes.

GOOD DEEDS WIPE OUT BAD ONES

The principle "good deeds wipe out bad ones" is clearly indicated in the following two ayāt of *Qur'an*:

$$ إِنَّ الْحَسَنَاتِ يُذْهِبْنَ السَّيِّئَاتِ $$

> . . . for those things that are good remove those that are evil. (11:114)

and:

> . . . and they turn off evil with good. (13:22)

It opens the door for repentance and correcting mistakes and bad deeds. This is also emphasized by the Prophet in the following hadith in which Abu Dhar Jundub ibn Junadah reports that the Messenger of Allah said:

> Have *taqwa* toward Allah wherever you are. Follow a bad deed with a good deed, so you may wipe it out. And deal with people using good manners.

Keep this principle in mind when you are dealing with your children. It is important to give them the opportunity to correct their mistakes through doing extra good deeds. As soon as the children do the extra good deed, parents should not remind them of their previous mistakes or keep mentioning their mistakes to them when they make new ones and are punished for them. It is important that as soon as the child is punished for his or her mistake that he or she should not be reminded of it repeatedly. It is a common negative parental behaviour to become historical as soon as their children make another mistake. Some of them may say, "remember on such and such date when you did this bad thing," or, "remember when you behaved badly during your uncle's visit," or, "remember when you didn't help your sister and were rude with her," etc. even though the child may have already been punished. This sort of action reduces children's self-esteem and makes them feel that their parents are picking on them. This is not what you want for your children; you are aspiring to make them strong and confident Muslims. Don't be picky and fussy with them, especially if they have already performed good deeds as an act of atonement. This is how to practice this wonderful principle with our children, and in conjunction with the previous principle of accountability, we can use them to help our children to be better and stronger Muslims.

EMPHASIS AND ENCOURAGEMENT

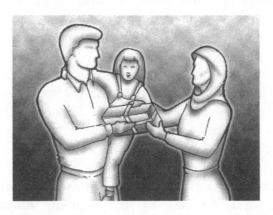

Children's efforts should be encouraged and applauded.

Emphasize positive actions performed by your children. Be reasonable in your expectations of them. Only request what is possible and within their ability.

Allah says:

$$\text{لا يُكَلِّفُ اللَّهُ نَفْسًا إِلا وُسْعَهَا}$$

Allah does not burden any soul with more than its capability. (2:286)

The Prophet is reported to have said:

Whatever I order you to do, do it as much as you can. And whatever I forbid you, avoid it completely." (Agreed upon)

A man came to the Prophet and asked him about Islam. The Prophet told him the basic pillars of Islam (five daily prayers, *zakah*, fasting, and *hajj*). The man said he will only do this and nothing more. The Prophet said that this man will achieve prosperity if he implements what he said.

The Prophet emphasized the positive aspect of the man's intention, encouraging him. He did not ask him to do more. Simply by starting to practice acts of worship in the proper way, one discovers its beauty and sweetness, and naturally desires to do more. If the Prophet had asked more of him, the man may have felt it is too much to do and perhaps would have given up, even before he could get started.

Parents, observe this principle during the *tarbiyah* process with your children. Ask them to do only what they are able and encourage them for their achievement. This is a great motivator and ensures high self-esteem, confidence, and helps children to be ready for new challenges.

Continue to encourage your children. For example, if they spend sometime coloring a picture, respond by saying, *"Masha' Allah,* you have spent all this time by yourself doing this nice coloring. That is great effort, my dear." Even if the colors were not the best or they were not within the boundaries of the picture, don't emphasize this; rather emphasize the effort that your child exerted in coloring the picture. It is a proven fact that emphasizing children's shortcomings discourages them from trying the same activity again.

Another common example of parents discouraging their children is the parents' response and their comments to children during prayer training. As a way of training, parents often ask their children to stay with them in the same line during the *jumu'ah* (group) prayer. Of course, children's span of attention is very short. It is very difficult for them to stand still for a long period of time; naturally, they move during such training. As soon as the prayer finishes, parents make a big mistake by reprimanding their children, saying, "How many times have I told you not to move during the prayer?" How discouraged your children become. Instead, say, "*Ma sha'a Allah* you were able to stand still during the whole first *rak'ah* of the prayer. This is good. *Insha'ā Allah,* next time you can do two *raka'ah*s" and so on.

DO THINGS STEP BY STEP AND CONSIDER YOUR CHILD'S LEVEL

Take a gradual step-by-step approach to your children's training. This is a basic principle in training and development. The *sirah* of the Prophet is full of examples supporting this concept. When the Prophet sent Mu'ādh ibn Jabal to Yemen, he told him to tell the people of Yemen to bear witness that there is no deity but Allah and that Muhammad is His messenger. Then the Prophet said, "If they accept this from you then tell them that Allah makes it obligatory on them to pray five times a day. If they accept this, tell them that Allah orders them to pay *zakah*. If they accept this, tell them that Allah orders them to fast the month of *Ramadan*." In this *hadith* the Prophet establishes the importance of introducing new concepts to people gradually and gently.

This principle is also demonstrated very clearly regarding the revealed injunctions prohibiting alcoholic beverages. In three or four stages, the *Qur'an* gradually revealed its ruling on alcohol, finally making it completely *haram*. First, the *Qur'an* hinted that things that make people drunk are not good:

$$\text{تَتَّخِذُونَ مِنْهُ سَكَرًا وَرِزْقًا حَسَنًا}$$

. . . From it you derive intoxicants as well as wholesome sustenance. (16:67)

In the second stage Allah says:

يَسْـأَلُونَكَ عَـنْ الْخَمْرِ وَالْمَيْسِرِ قُـلْ فِيهِمَا إِثْمٌ كَبِيرٌ وَمَنَافِعُ لِلنَّـاسِ
وَإِثْمُهُمَا أَكْبَرُ مِنْ نَفْعِهِمَا

They will ask you about intoxicants and games of chance. Say: In
both there is great evil as well as some benefit for people; but the
evil which they cause is greater than the benefit which they bring.
(2:219)

The *Qur'an* is indicating that the harms of drinking are much more
than the benefits.

The third stage came when Allah says in the *Qur'an*:

يَاأَيُّهَا الَّذِينَ آمَنُوا لا تَقْرَبُـوا الصَّلاةَ وَأَنْتُـمْ سُكَارَى حَتَّى تَعْلَمُـوا مَـا
تَقُولُونَ وَلا جُنُبًا إلا عَابِرِي سَبِيلٍ حَتَّى تَغْتَسِـلُوا

O You who believe! Do not attempt to pray while you are in a
state of drunkenness, (but wait) until you know what you are saying; nor yet (while you are) in a state requiring total ablution,
until you have bathed . . . (4:43)

In the final stage Allah says:

يَاأَيُّهَا الَّذِينَ آمَنُوا إِنَّمَا الْخَمْرُ وَالْمَيْسِرُ وَالانصَابُ وَالازْلامُ رِجْـسٌ مِـنْ
عَمَلِ الشَّيْطَانِ فَاجْتَنِبُوهُ لَعَلَّكُمْ تُفْلِحُونَ

O You who have attained to faith! Intoxicants, and games of
chance, and idolatrous practices, and the divining of the future
are but a loathsome evil of Satan's doing: shun it then, so that you
might attain to a happy state! (5:90)

Every stage played an important role in preparing the human nature of the believers to accept the final prohibition. It took a few years to turn the companions from this social habit.

Parents should also be gradual when trying to change the behavior of their children. Do not expect miracles. Behavioral change is not a simple matter. It takes time and requires persistence, repeated trials, and gradual gains.

For example, your children may be used to going to bed every night at 11:00 PM. This is a bad habit, and as a parent you should change it. Children need enough sleep during the night to be fully responsive and active during the day and to pay good attention to their lessons in school. To change this habit, don't force your children to go to bed at 8:00 PM all at once—it will be very difficult to implement. Rather use gradual change. First, ask your children to go to bed at 10:30 PM. Continue this for a week. Then set another time such as 10:00 PM for another week and so on, until they reach their target of 8:00 PM.

EXPRESSING FEELINGS AND SHARING HAPPINESS AND PAIN

Allow your children to express their feelings and share their happiness and pains. This is a very important principle in children's *tarbiyah*. If parents successfully encourage their children to express their feelings, when a problem arises, their children will always come back to them seeking their help. When parents do not allow their children to express their feelings, the children will keep them to themselves. This is a serious mistake that many parents fall into, and creates a big communication gap between them and their children. Children have to find a way to express their feelings to their parents, otherwise, they will find others to talk to—teachers, councilors, friends, or their peers, who could mislead them. They may begin to hide their emotions from their parents, thus leading to serious future problems—not listening to their parents, not consulting them when they have problems. The Prophet allowed young children to express their feelings. Actually, he even acknowledged these feelings and shared them with them. It is reported that one day the Prophet came to the house of Abu Bakr and found 'A'ishah behind a door weeping. He asked her for the reason and she complained about her mother. In sympathy, the Prophet cried with her and talked to her mother to solve the problem. See how the Prophet of Allah shared the feelings of 'A'ishah, who was six years old then! How do you apply this principle with your children? Let us give you a simple example to illustrate.

Suppose your child come back from school one day in a bad mood, complaining that he had a problem with some of his peers. Some parents may directly respond to their child by saying, "This is not a problem. You are a big boy now and you shouldn't worry about these small things," without allowing him to express his feelings. This is not the right approach to solve the problem. As a parent, you should try to use the prophetic methodology. Ask the child to describe the problem for you and show sympathy towards him. This can be done through the following steps:

˘ Leave the task you are currently involved in and give him your undivided attention

˘ Turn towards him fully and listen attentively to what he says. Observe his body language and make note of the tone of his voice.

˘ Tell him that you would have felt the same way if such a thing happened to you.

˘ Ask him if he wants you to interfere to help in resolving the problem or talk to the school administration, if the situation warrants such an action.

˘ If he says (No), he will try to deal with the problem himself, suggest that you can brainstorm together various ideas and approaches to deal with the problem and let him choose, with your guidance, the most suitable one.

˘ Assure him that you are there for him if he changes his mind and wants you to interfere on his behalf.

This way, you've shared his feelings, helped him analyze the problem and guided him through the pros and cons of each suggestion. This is a valuable exercise for your child. The time you spend with him is very well spent time and he will appreciate your understanding and support during this hard time. All that he needed was to feel your support and encouragement.

You should also share every happy occasion with your child and make him feel that you are as happy as he is. It is also your happiness, no matter how small or large the occasion is, starting from an improvement in his marks in some subject tests and ending by being accepted into the most prestigious university.

Sharing such pains and happiness creates a very strong bond which helps greatly in keeping a healthy and open channel of communication between you and your child.

BEING CLEAR IN COMMUNICATION

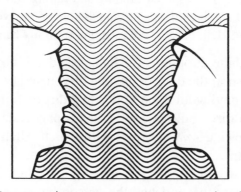

Parents on the same communication's wavelength

It is related from 'A'ishah that the Messenger of Allah spoke clearly so that all those who listened to him would understand him (Abu Dawud).

Anas relates that the Messenger of Allah used to repeat his words thrice so that their meanings were understood fully. (Bukhari)

When the Prophet wanted to deliver a message he would attract people's attention in various ways. Commonly, he would start with a question. It is reported that the Prophet began speaking with the question, "Do you know who the bankrupt person is?"

During the Farewell Hajj, he started his speech by asking the congregation, "Do you know which day this is? Do you know which month this is? Do you know which year this is?"

To attract people's attention, the Prophet would also give examples. The Prophet is reported to have said,

> The believers, in their mutual kindness, compassion, and sympathy, are like one body. If one of the organs is afflicted, the whole body responds to it with wakefulness and fever. (Agreed upon)

He also said:

> I and you are like someone who has ignited a fire into which moths and other insects have started running and falling and who is trying to stop them. I am like this man trying to hold you by your waists (to save you) from Hell, but you are escaping from my hands. (Muslim)

Muhammad, the Prophet of Allah, asked his companions, "If there was a river at the door of anyone of you and he took a bath in it five times a day, would you notice any dirt on him?" They said, "Not a trace of dirt would be left." The Prophet added, "That is the example of the five *salah* prayers with which Allah blots out evil deeds" (Muslim).

The Prophet would often explain the logic behind his argument in a convincing way that touched the person he was talking to. The following is reported:

> When a young man came to the Prophet asking permission to fornicate, the Prophet told him, "Would you like it for your mother?" The man said, "No." He asked him, "Would you like it for your sister?" The young man said, "No." He asked him, "Would you like it for your aunt?" He said, "No." He asked him, "Would you like it for your cousin?" He said, "No." Then the Prophet told him, "Likewise, people would not like it for their female relatives." And he put his hand on the young man's chest and prayed that Allah grants him chastity.

See how the Prophet discussed the matter logically with the young man and gave him a clear explanation that touched him.

Follow this principle with everybody and especially with children. They deserve to have a proper explanation that suites their level of understanding.

Good, clear communication with the child achieves long-lasting closeness and ensures great bonding between the child and the parents. Certain times of the day are more effective than others for building this bond. Among these special times are the early mornings when the child wakes up, after school when the child comes home, at the dinner table, and before going to bed. Parents should prepare themselves to make the best of these times and utilize them properly. The early morning is a great time to bond, so parents should wake up early with their children and spend time with them as they prepare for school. In addition to encouraging and supporting comments parents can give their children to help start their day with the right attitude, the early morning is the most suitable time for memorizing the *Qur'an* and learning *du'a*s. This can be done while they are getting ready for school, even if it is only for a few minutes. At this time children are well rested and their minds are clear and more receptive for memorization. Being warm and loving to them at this time is important because it gives them a positive feeling as they are leaving to face the day.

When your kids come home from school, be prepared to listen to them to find out how they did at school. At this time you will be able to share their feelings if they faced any problems during the school day. At the dinner table, it is time for each member of the family to speak about his/her day. The dad or mom might start the conversation and the children would follow. As for bedtime, this is storytelling time. It helps if both mom and dad take turns in storytelling before bed. Stories about the life of the Prophet, his companions, prophets in general and Muslim heroes, as well as simple stories to teach good manners are the most suitable type of stories for children to hear before going to sleep. Other stories to deal with certain problems can also be told. See section 4 for more details on storytelling.

The effectiveness of the above times depends on the child's age. While the morning and bedtimes are more effective for young children and children in their early school years, directly after school and dinnertime are much more effective for teenagers and children in their middle school years.

Keeping an open channel of communication with your child when he/she is young, is a great investment for the teenage years. The nature and type of communication will vary according to the child's age and needs. For a baby or an infant, kissing, hugging, and tickling are all good ways of communication. For a toddler, story-telling at bedtime, songs, and family games provide more ways of communication. In later years, going out to the park with the child and playing a ball game is a very effective way of communication. In such a setting, the child feels more at ease, and talks to parents about any concerns he/she may have. All these ways help in establishing a great bond between the child and parents and enhancing the quality of their communication and mutual respect.

ACTIVE LISTENING

Active listening is the listener's attempt to restate the feeling and/or content of what the speaker has said. The listener tries to understand how it feels to be the other person. Implied is the other person's worth in attention and in time.

Active listening cannot be faked. It demands more than just nodding the head and an occasional "uh-huh." Active listening is difficult because it demands that you understand another person's communication and that you suspend judgment of what is being said. By withholding judgment you communicate respect to the other person. Empathy builds trust.

The Prophet is a good example of an active listener, even with his enemies and those who disagreed with him.

As parents, active listening is a great quality that we should develop when dealing with our children. It will earn their trust and help strengthen our relationships with them.

Find Suitable Alternatives

Healthy recreational alternatives

In the West, it is the parents' responsibility to find proper recreational alternatives to fill their children's lives, and to replace the bad influence of destructive social habits and television. When the Prophet came to Madinah, he found that they had two annual days of celebration and feasting. He told them that Allah has replaced these two days for them with two better days—the two *'Īds*, *'Īd al Aḍḥa* and *'Īd al Fitr*. You see, to change a certain bad habit, the Prophet did more than order Muslims to avoid it, he offered a substitute superior to what they were asked to leave!

Here is an example on how to use this principle with your children:

There is no doubt that most of us would like to minimize the number of hours our children spend watching television or surfing the internet. To do this we have to provide a better alternative, such as Islamic videos. It is encouraging that Alhamdulillah nowadays, we can find good, high quality Islamic videos compared to a few years ago. Although parents should use these videos with their children, we would like them to observe the following points:

˘ Don't make the Islamic video another passive watching activity for your children. Set with them and make it an enjoyable learning experience for both of you and an opportunity for bonding and discussion

ˇ Don't allow your children to keep watching the same videos repeatedly. It is better to provide other alternatives that give them the chance to be active participants, such as:
- Going out together for hiking or bicycle trips
- Being part of the community soccer/sports teams
- Going out for picnics
- Camping
- Etc.

Please make sure that the Islamic video your children are watching is a legal copy. Do not copy videos illegally from friends or allow them to copy from your legally bought video. In addition to the fact that it is illegal to do this, it also contributes negatively to the financial well being of the Islamic video producers. This may seriously impact their ability to continue producing the clean, useful alternative for our children.

ASSIST IN SKILL DEVELOPMENT

As parents, our responsibility is to help our children attain the proper survival skills suitable for their environment and time. 'Umar ibn al Khattab is reported to have said, "Teach your children swimming, shooting, and horseback riding." Also it was narrated in Tabarany that the prophet may Allah's peace and blessings be upon him has said:" Every activity other than Allah's remembrance is considered a waste of time except four activities: When a man is training for shooting, when a man is domesticating his horse, when a man is entertaining his family, and when a man is teaching his children swimming." It was also narrated in the authentic collection of Imam Muslim may Allah be pleased with him that the Prophet pbuh recited the verse: "And prepare against them the utmost force you can." (Q 8, V 60), then said: "Truly, power is in being a good shooter, truly power is in being a good shooter, truly power is in being a good shooter." He also, may Allah's peace and blessings be upon him, as narrated in the authentic collection of Imam Al-Bukhari, encouraged his companions to be good shooters and use to tell them during their training; "Improve your shooting skills and I'm with you."

These skills were the survival skills needed for their environment. We can't limit the meaning of the Prophet's teaching to these three skills only. Our children need the skills that give them empowerment in Western society—Self-defence, the skill of being able to make choices, sports, administrative skills, computer skills, communication skills, business skills, and so on.

Let us elaborate on how we can we teach our children at least one of these skills. First, we would like to point out that such a process should start at a very early age of the child's life. For example, if you want your child to grow up with the ability to make decisions and choose the right alternative when he is faced with making such choices, you have to provide the needed training for him. This is a very important quality, because life is all about making the right choices. Rather than, because you are in rush, dressing your three old boy in any outfit, it may be better to take two outfits from the closet, put them on the bed and ask him: Which of these would you like to wear? and let him make his own choice. You can also ask your four year old daughter: Would you like to have pasta and meatballs for dinner tonight, or would you rather have chicken and rice? You can ask your six year-old child: where do you want to spend Saturday? Would like to visit your friend Hasan or would you rather we go to the park? You can also ask your eight year-old daughter: Would you like that we alternate reading *Qur'an* together? Or; do you prefer to read while I listen to your reading? Your teen should be involved in making decisions with you in various matters related to family affairs and activities, such as a long trip to visit one of the Muslim countries, deciding on where you are going to spend the summer vacation, moving to a new house, etc. Giving these kinds of choices in simple matters related to the child's environment and suitable to his/her age will help him/her to develop the ability to make decisions, which is a very important skill for every individual.

When he grows up in his teens years, if he is pressured by one of his peers to smoke, for example, he will be able to make the right choice and say NO to his friend because he already knows how to chose between alternatives. He already went through the training early in his life and is able to make decisions based on the right information.

A child who was never given the chance to make his own choice while he was young, will be very vulnerable in front of peer pressure and most of the time he would be a follower. He is trying to fit in, and it will be very difficult for him to say NO to his peers with confidence and without feeling defeated.

It is our duty as parents to provide such training to ensure that our Muslim teens are strong, confident, and will not yield to the first peer pressure they face insha'a Allah. One of the most important principles to ensure this healthy development is to help them in being capable and skilled Muslims

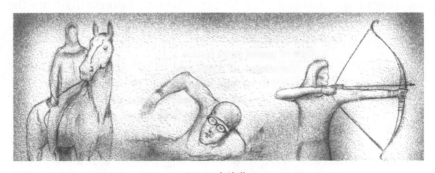

Survival Skills

CONTROLLING ANGER

Among the many pieces of advice given to us by the Prophet is the advice to not become angry. The following is narrated by Abu Hurayrah:

A man asked the Messenger of Allah to give him a piece of advice. He said, "Don't become angry." The man repeated his question several times and the Prophet gave the same reply, "Don't become angry." (Bukhari)

The Prophet defined the strong man as the one who controls himself when he is angry, and not the one who wrestles others.

Mu'adh ibn Anas narrates that the Prophet said:

The one who swallows up anger, will be called out by Allah, the Exalted, to the forefront of the creatures on Resurrection Day and will be offered any pure-eyed virgin he will like. (Abu Dawud and Al Tirmidhi)

Don't be like this with your children

Not only did the Prophet warn us about getting angry, but he also taught us the best anger management techniques. They are as follows:

- SEEK REFUGE WITH ALLAH FROM SATAN:

  Sulayman ibn Surd relates that two people began to quarrel in front of the Prophet. The face of one of them turned red and the veins of his neck were swollen. The Messenger of Allah said, "I know of a phrase that if he were to utter it, his fit of rage would abate. The phrase is 'I seek refuge with Allah from Satan, the accursed.'" So the companions said to him, "The Messenger of Allah has said, 'Seek refuge with Allah from Satan, the outcast.'" (Agreed upon)

- CHANGE YOUR POSITION:

  It was narrated that the Messenger of Allah said, "If one of you gets angry while he is standing let him sit down, and if he is still angry let him lie down" (Ahmad).

- PERFORM *WUDU*:

It was narrated that the Prophet said, "Anger is from Satan, Satan is created from fire, and fire is extinguished by water, so if one of you becomes angry let him perform *wuḍu*" (Abu Dawud).

• BE SILENT:

It was narrated that the Prophet said, "If one of you gets angry let him be silent" (Ahmad).

When you are in conflict with your children, make use of all these wonderful techniques for managing your anger. Do not be quick to react when you are upset with your kids, instead use one of the above strategies. It may be difficult at first, it does take training, but these techniques are very helpful and make it a lot easier to avoid unnecessary problems. Teach your children these anger management techniques, and train them to use them.

HELP YOUR CHILDREN COOPERATE WITH YOU

The *Qur'an* tells us in *surah Ṣāffāt* about the story of the Prophet Ibrāhīm and his son, the Prophet Ismāʿīl, peace be upon them both:

فَبَشَّرْنَاهُ بِغُلَامٍ حَلِيمٍ فَلَمَّا بَلَغَ مَعَهُ السَّعْيَ قَالَ يَابُنَيَّ إِنِّي أَرَى فِي الْمَنَامِ أَنِّي أَذْبَحُكَ فَانظُرْ مَاذَا تَرَى قَالَ يَاأَبَتِ افْعَلْ مَا تُؤْمَرُ سَتَجِدُنِي إِنْ شَاءَ اللَّهُ مِنْ الصَّابِرِينَ

So we gave him the good news of a forbearing son. Then, when (the son) reached [the age of serious] work with him, he said: "O my son! I have seen in a dream that I offer you in sacrifice. Now see what is your view?" (The son) said: "O my father! Do as you are commanded. You will find me, if Allah so wills, one of the steadfast." (37:101–102)

Although it was an order from Allah to the Prophet Ibrāhīm, he still consulted his son Ismāʿīl before executing the order. This should serve as a great lesson for all parents. When parents consult with their children (or child), the children feel that they are part of what is going on. It is much more effective than just giving orders because the consultation process itself is a learning experience for children. From consultation, children establish priorities and learn decision making skills that help them for the rest of their lives. Also, children feel a greater sense of responsibility and conviction to carry out their part in the agreement if they have discussed and agreed to it. Of course, the parents' guidance, follow-up, and supervision are always needed. This process can start at a very early age. For example, you can ask your children what they would like to eat for dinner: pasta and meatballs or chicken and rice? Or you can ask them whether they would like to read the *Qur'an* together, or read while you listen? Offering choices in simple matters related to the children's environment helps them develop the ability to make decisions, which is a very important skill for every individual. It also helps them to carry out their end of the agreement.

ALWAYS FULFILL A PROMISE

Fulfilling a promise is one of the great virtues in Islam. The *Qur'an* emphasizes this fact, such as in the following two verses:

$$\text{يَاأَيُّهَا الَّذِينَ آمَنُوا أَوْفُوا بِالْعُقُودِ}$$

O you who believe, fulfill (all) obligations. (5:1)

$$\text{وَالْمُوفُونَ بِعَهْدِهِمْ إِذَا عَاهَدُوا}$$

To fulfill the contracts which you have made . . ." (2:177)

In *surah Mariam* the Qur'an praises the Prophet Ismā'īl for always fulfilling his promise:

$$\text{وَاذْكُرْ فِي الْكِتَابِ إِسْمَاعِيلَ إِنَّهُ كَانَ صَادِقَ الْوَعْدِ وَكَانَ رَسُولًا نَبِيًّا}$$

Also mention in the Book (the story of) Ismāʿīl: he was (strictly) true to what he promised, and he was a messenger (and) a prophet." (19:54)

Also in *surah Mu'minūn*, the Qur'an promises those who fulfill their promises with success and prosperity:

$$\text{وَالَّذِينَ هُمْ لِأَمَانَاتِهِمْ وَعَهْدِهِمْ رَاعُونَ}$$

Those who faithfully observe their trusts and their covenants. (23:8)

The teachings of the Prophet Muhammad are full of advice and illustrative examples related to keeping promises. On one occasion the Prophet saw a lady asking her son to come to her with her hands closed, "If you come to me I'll give you [so and so]." The Prophet told her, "If you don't give him what you promise, this will be counted against you as a lie."

From this event, we learn that before making a promise, you must first consider if it is within your reach. For example, don't promise your child something lavish, knowing that it might be difficult to buy.

It is of great importance to children's personality development that if parents promise them something that they should try their best to fulfill it. Sometimes parents use promises to get themselves out of certain situations with children without thinking about it or having the intention to fulfill such promises. This is a huge mistake on the parents' part. Only promise what you can fulfill and don't use promises as bribes.

For instance, if you want your children to memorize Qur'an, make sure you have explained to them why this is important. Don't just promise material things as a reward. Although there is nothing wrong with using gifts as encouragement, a more productive method is to promise them an hour of quality time in the park or a visit to a friend's house when they have finished the task. Be sure that your children are always aware that the real reward is from

Allah and remind them of this whenever you are giving them the immediate material reward.

Another point to emphasize here is the light threats that some parents direct at their children to get out of certain situation or to keep them quite. Sometimes, parents take these threats to the extreme without thinking about whether or not they can come through on them. For example, if the family is driving on the highway and one of the kids is making noise, a parent may say, "Hasan, If you don't stop the noise you are making at once, I'll stop the car and leave you here alone on the road!!!" No parent will ever be able to implement this action. As such, the child will not trust his parent or take him seriously because he failed to follow up on his threat since it was irrational. Thus, it is very important to make sure you only use rational punishments which can be implemented without harm.

FOLLOW UP ON ORDERS AND BE CONSISTENT

Various Qur'anic commandments did not just come once, they were repeated and emphasized over and over again in different ways. This indicates the importance of following up. In the Qur'an, Allah says:

$$ وَأْمُرْ أَهْلَكَ بِالصَّلَاةِ وَاصْطَبِرْ عَلَيْهَا $$

And enjoin your people with prayer and be constant on it. (20:132)

Again this shows the importance of being constant and repeating the same order.

The word *Wastaber* in the Arabic language used in the above verse is not only taken from the root word sabr, but it is also expressed with very strong emphasis. This indicates that parents should never give up. They should try every possible way to train their children to do the right thing and adhere to Islamic values.

If one method of training hasn't worked, they have to think of other methods and keep trying without giving up.

It should be noted here that the methods used by parents should suit their children's age. For example, with younger children, story telling in a casual, informal, and warm atmosphere is very well suited to teaching them certain values and moral characteristics. Follow up with the children on the characteristic they have just learned from the story is a must; otherwise, they may not implement what they have learned.

Let's illustrate this with a practical example; say the children have just been taught about the characteristic of respecting others. If parents notice that their child is behaving in a disrespectful way towards adults, such as talking to his father in a sharp or rude tone or using unacceptable expressions like, "I don't care" etc. what should they do? They should follow up using these steps:

ˇ Firstly, whoever is dealing with the situation should try not to react directly to the child's behavior. He should keep quiet for a while, try to control his anger and become calm. Never react out of anger.

ˇ Secondly, he should call his child to a private area of the house and speak to him in a firm, assertive, but not angry tone. He should explain to him that the way he/she behaved is improper. All of this should be done in a polite and respectful manner, and the parent should point this out to his child. He might even ask the child, "Am I speaking to you in a rude way right now? No. I'm speaking to you calmly and respectfully." He should also remind his child of the saying of Prophet Muhammad PBUH, "He is not from us the one who does not respect our elders and the one who has no mercy on our young ones." The parent should ask his child to ask Allah's forgiveness for his sin. Then, he should tell him to please repeat his disrespectful action in a proper way, without using unacceptable expressions or a rude tone of voice.

ˇ Thirdly, when the child does as he/she is told, his parent should thank him/her and remind him/her not to repeat the disrespectful behaviour or there will be consequences.

ˇ Fourthly, after the child modifies his/her behaviour, it is important that parents not insult or humiliate him/her over the incident.
It is also important not to remind him/her of his/her mistakes
regularly.

ˇ Fifthly, if the same behaviour recurs, parents should repeat the
process, and this time, they may add certain disciplinary measures
to follow up on their promise that actions have certain consequences and bad behavior can't go unpunished. These measures
could include depriving the child from certain privileges, such as
not allowing him/her to visit his/her friend for a week or not letting
him/her go to the community picnic, etc.

You should also use some tools to help you, as a parent, in the
process of follow up. These could be follow-up charts displayed in
an agreed-upon location in the house (such as on the fridge), or
written contracts.

Parents must observe this principle. When you instruct your child
to do something, even something little, be serious and make sure
you make eye contact. If the child does not carry out the instruction,
repeat it again in a firm and serious voice but never lose your
temper or shout.

When you say it only once and the child doesn't do it, ignoring
the fact that nothing was done has serious consequences. From then
on, the child will always take your instructions lightly. However, if
you follow it up, the child will understand that you mean business,
and will take it seriously.

This principle applies to every instruction because it serves to
build good habits, starting from cleaning up after eating or
playing to putting on the seat belt in the car to praying on time.
In the seat belt case if you ignore enforcing it the consequences
may be deadly.

TEACH THEM *HAYA'*

It was reported that the Prophet said, "For every *dīn,* there is a
principle attribute, and the attribute of Islam is *haya'.*" The Prophet
was described as having more *haya'* than a virgin in her private

hiding place. Although *haya'* is usually translated as modesty, certainly, it is much more than just this. It is also shyness whenever it is proper, bashfulness, and completely avoiding any obscene talk or actions.

North American culture does not promote *haya'* at all. Most news magazines, TV programs and even commercials are full of unacceptable scenes which promote obscenity and low moral values. The behavioral norms are drastically declining. As Muslims, we should not follow the crowd and accept these norms. It is absolutely critical that parents protect their children from the low moral values that are fully accepted by the North American society. The Clinton/Monica Lewinsky episode is a good example of this low moral standard. Even after her testimony and his confession, 62 percent of the American people still saw nothing wrong with what their president did. How low can the norm of moral values go?

Teaching *haya'* should begin early in children's lives. Before they are two years old, don't expose them while changing their diapers or getting them ready for a bath by having them walk through the living room naked. This will indicate to the child that we only take our clothes off in private. When your children start going to school or visiting friends' houses, give them clear instruction that they should have no one accompanying them in the washroom. While watching TV, train your child to turn it off whenever there are obscene language or scenes. While you are doing this, you should remind your children that Allah will ask us how we used the senses He has granted us. Accompany your reminder with the verse:

$$\text{إِنَّ السَّمْعَ وَالْبَصَرَ وَالْفُؤَادَ كُلُّ أُوْلَئِكَ كَانَ عَنْهُ مَسْئُولًا}$$

Every act of hearing or of seeing or of feeling in the heart will be inquired into. (17:36)

USE EXAMPLES FROM THEIR ENVIRONMENT

The Prophet of Allah taught by using examples in the immediate environment to make sure that the audience understood clearly what he meant. It is reported that the Prophet said, "If the hour is about to happen and one of you has a small plant in his hands and he is able to plant it, let him plant it." It is also reported by Abu Musa al-Ash'ari that the Messenger of Allah said,

> The likeness of the believer who recites the Holy Qur'an is that of a citron which has a sweet fragrance and delicious taste. A believer who does not recite the Holy Qur'an is like a date which has no fragrance but has a sweet taste. The likeness of a hypocrite who recites the Holy Qur'an is that of the colocynth which is fragrant but bitter. The hypocrite who does not recite the Holy Qur'an is like the basil which has no fragrance and is also bitter. (Agreed upon)

On the authority of Ibn 'Umar it is reported that the Messenger of Allah said, "The likeness of the one who knows the Qur'an well is as the likeness of the owner of camels: if he undertakes (reading and applying) it (the Qur'an), he will keep it, and if he sets it free (ignores the Qur'an), it goes away" (agreed upon). On the authority of Sahl bin Sa'd who reported that the Messenger of Allah said to 'Ali, "By Allah, if a single person is guided to Allah through you, it will be better for you than the red camels" (agreed upon).

It is clear from the above teachings of the Prophet may Allah's peace and blessing be upon him that the type of fruits, vegetables, and animals he spoke about in his examples were very well known to the common people who lived in the Arabian peninsula.

Using examples from the immediate environment clarifies the issue under discussion and brings closeness among people. It is important for parents to use examples from their children's environment while they are interacting with them — especially when dealing with teenagers. Obviously, this imposes a great responsibility on parents; they should understand the North American environment, know what it calls for, adopt what is good, and reject what is bad.

The following are a few examples to illustrate this principle:

a) One example that worked very well for our daughter when we were explaining to her the meaning of the Day of Judgment is the following: Suppose you have a quiz to study for, how long in advance will you prepare? What if you have a test? Do you then prepare farther ahead of time? What if you have an important end-of-year exam? Think of your life as the study period you have before the most enormous exam you can imagine — the day of judgment. Don't you need to prepare for it?

b) A good analogy to use with your children when you are explaining why they should pay attention to their level of spirituality as much as they pay attention to their material possessions is this: When people in this society want to buy a stereo system, they call all the stores that sell them, find out about all the different prices of all the different models. They find out what the best buy is in terms of quality and price, and only when they are completely satisfied do they buy it. But a lot of them don't pay attention to anything spiritual. They don't read their holy book. They don't go to church. Look how much these people care about their material belongings. Isn't your emotional and spiritual well-being more important than that? If someone has all the money in the world, that person still can't buy peace of mind. But people who are content with their life will be happy even if they are sick or poor, because they know that they will be going to a better place after this life.

USE A HOLISTIC APPROACH

Islam approaches the question of *tarbiyyah* in a holistic way. It touches every side of the human being to make sure that this *tarbiyyah* produces a well-rounded person who is justly balanced and moderate in his/her behavior. In *surah Baqarah*, Allah says:

$$\text{يَاأَيُّهَا الَّذِينَ آمَنُوا ادْخُلُوا فِي السِّلْمِ كَافَّةً}$$

O you who believe, enter Islam in totality. (2:208)

In the same *surah,* the *Qur'an* talks about those who believe in part of the scripture and don't believe in other parts in a very humiliating way, and promises them severe punishment. This is an indication that Muslims should take Islam as a complete package.

We should not pick and choose only what is convenient and easy to apply from Islam and leave other issues that may cause us some inconvenience.

One of the common mistakes of some parents in North America is the unbalanced approach in *tarbiyyah*. For example, some emphasize the issue of wearing a *hijab* and do nothing else to prepare their daughters for womanhood. Yes, wearing a *hijab* is important, but making sure that your daughters are convinced that it is the right thing is even more important. Using a comprehensive approach in *tarbiyyah* is very important in producing the right outcome. Islam respects thinking and encourages questioning to reach the right conclusion and to know the reason beyond certain prohibitions. Forcing children to do something without convincing them that it is the right thing may prove to be very costly in the future when they reach maturity and have the right to choose their way without parents' intervention.

To avoid this, make sure that your approach to *tarbiyyah* is a well-rounded one that covers various aspects and meets your children's various physical, emotional, and spiritual needs. Use stories, videos, Islamic camps, conferences, and other tools at your disposal.

Summary

In this chapter, we discussed the basic principles of *Tarbiyah*. We indicated the source of each principle from *Qur'an* and/or the teachings of Prophet Mohammad, may Allah's peace and blessings be upon him, and we provided a practical example on how to use these principles with your children. We covered the topic of understanding your children by knowing their basic needs, basic qualities and the key factors affecting the formation of their personality. Other principles and methods of training were also discussed. These principles and methods include:
– Linking the child to Allah
– The use of mercy, gentleness, kindness, and love
– Brevity in preaching
– Never resorting to force

- Fairness
- Every soul is accountable for what it earns
- Good deeds wipe out bad ones
- Emphasizing positive action
- Using a step by step approach
- Sharing feelings
- Active listening
- Developing skills
- Providing suitable alternatives
- Controlling anger
- Teaching cooperation
- Fulfilling promises
- Following up and being consistent
- Teaching *Haya*
- Using examples from the environment
- Using a holistic approach

CHAPTER 3

ENVIRONMENT

INTRODUCTION

This chapter is devoted to a discussion of the social environment,
its importance, and its impact on our children. We will look at
the differences between the parents' environment and the children's
environment, the problems and pressures our children face in
North America, and the parents' responsibility to foster a positive
environment. We suggest what parents can do to minimize the
negative impact environment has on their children, or at least to
neutralize the environment and reduce its hostility toward them.

IMPORTANCE OF ENVIRONMENT

On the authority of Abu Sa'id Sa'd bin Malek bin Sinan Al-Khu-
dri (may Allah be pleased with him) who narrated that the   messenger of Allah (may the peace and blessings of Allah be upon him)
had said, "There was a person before you, who killed ninety nine
persons then inquired about the most learned person of the world,
who could show him the path for salvation. He was directed to go
to a monk. He came to him and told him that he had killed ninety-
nine persons and asked him if there was any scope for his repentance to be accepted. He said: No. So, the man killed the monk,
completing the number to one hundred. He then asked about
the most learned person of the earth. He was directed to go to a
scholar. He told him that he had killed one hundred persons and he

asked him if there was any chance for his repentance to be accept-ed. He said: Yes, and who can stand between you and repentance? **You should proceed to such and such land; there are people devoted to prayer and worship, and you should join them in worship; and don't come back to your land because it is an evil place (for you).** So the man went away and hardly had he covered half the distance when death overtook him. Then there was a dispute between the angels of mercy and the angels of torment. The angels of mercy said: This man has come as a repentant to Allah. The angels of punishment said: he has done no good at all. Then there appeared another angel in the form of a human being (to decide the issue). The contending angels agreed that he should act as an arbiter between them. He said: Measure the distance between the two lands. He will possess that land to which he is near. They measured and found him closer to the land where he intended to go and so the angels of mercy grasped him (agreed upon)

Note that the scholar's advice to the man is to proceed to another land and leave his land because it is evil for him. This means that the scholar advised him to change his current environment, which has a bad influence on him, to a better environment. This is the first step on the road to salvation and repentance. A better environment is clearly needed to help a person not to fall into the same mistakes and commit similar sins again. The above teaching of the Prophet PBUH is full of great lessons for us and among them, it emphasizes the effect of the environment on people's behaviour and the importance of ensuring the proper positive environment so as to have a lasting impact on the characteristics and morals of those who live in such an environment.

Here is another very clear life example illustrating the effect of the environment on people's behaviour. Consider the situation when you are trying to park your car next to another car, which is parked in a crooked way, or not exactly parallel to the parking lines. No matter how hard you try, most of the time you will end up parking your car not-quite parallel to the marks of the parking spot because you are subconsciously using the other car as a guide for yourself while you park. This indicates clearly that our environment has a great impact on us and we really have to work hard to either ensure the presence of a proper environment for our children or to counter the negative impact of the environment on them, as explained in other sections of this chapter later *insha'a Allah*.

The importance of a proper environment for bringing up children cannot be overemphasized. The Prophet indicated that the human being is born in a state of pure, original nature, and it is his parents who make him Jewish, Christian, or Magian.

Here is how some scholars have interpereted this great hadith:

1. It is clear that "pure, original nature" represents Islam without any distortions. If a newborn baby were to be left alone without external religious influences (stimuli), it would eventually quite readily recognize the Oneness of God.
2. The environment has a great impact on the way a child is brought up.
3. Parents represent the first circle of environment faced by a child. This circle is so important that it can change a child's pure, original nature by its influence.

Other environmental circles which children face are schools, neighbors, and friends (local community). In general, mainstream society is represented in all the events, ideas, and information that are dumped on children via the media—particularly, the television.

Here is a beautiful and relevant story I received one day through my email. The story goes like this:

A few months before I was born, my dad met a stranger who was new to our small Tennessee town. From the beginning, Dad was fascinated with this enchanting newcomer, and soon invited him to live with our family.

The stranger was quickly accepted and was around to welcome me into the world a few months later. As I grew up I never questioned his place in our family. In my young mind, each member had a special niche. My brother, Bill, five years my senior, was my example. Fran, my younger sister, gave me an opportunity to play big brother and develop the art of teasing. My parents were complementary instructors—Mom taught me to love the Word of God, and Dad taught me to obey it. But, the stranger was our storyteller. He could weave the most fascinating tales. Adventures, mysteries, and comedies were daily conversations. He could hold our whole family spellbound for hours each evening. If I wanted to know about politics, history, or science, he knew it all. He knew about the past, understood the present, and seemingly could predict the future. The pictures he could draw were so lifelike that I would often laugh or cry. He was like a friend to the whole family. He took Dad, Bill and me to our first major league baseball game. He was always encouraging us to see the movies and he even made arrangements to introduce us to several movie stars. My brother and I were deeply impressed by John Wayne in particular.

The stranger was an incessant talker. Dad didn't seem to mind, but sometimes Mom would quietly get up while the rest of us were enthralled with one of his stories of faraway places, go to her room, read her Bible and pray. I wonder now if she ever prayed that the stranger would leave.

You see, my dad ruled our household with certain moral convictions. But this stranger never felt an obligation to honor them. Profanity, for example, was not allowed in our house—not from us, from our friends, or adults. Our longtime visitor, however, used occasional four-letter words that burned my ears and made Dad squirm. To my knowledge the stranger was never confronted.

My dad was a teetotaler who didn't permit alcohol in his home—not even for cooking. But the stranger felt like we needed exposure and enlightened us to other ways of life. He offered us beer and other alcoholic beverages often. He made cigarettes look tasty, cigars manly, and pipes distinguished.

He talked freely (probably too much too freely) about sex. His comments were sometimes blatant, sometimes suggestive, and generally embarrassing. I know now that my early concepts of the man-woman relationship were influenced by the stranger.

As I look back, I believe it was the grace of God that the stranger did not influence us more. Time after time he opposed the values of my parents. Yet he was seldom rebuked and never asked to leave.

More than 30 years have passed since the stranger moved in with the young family on Morningside Drive. He is not nearly so intriguing to my Dad as he was in those early years.

But, if you were to walk into my parents den today, you would still see him sitting over in a corner, waiting for someone to listen to him talk and look at his pictures. His name?

We always just called him TV.

Television should be treated as a stranger, yet most families are treating it as a very close friend. They spent lots of time in front of the tube and some of them even use it as a babysitter. Doing this has dangerous consequences on children's behavior. The consequences might be related to various issues, such as violence, use of obscene language, promiscuity, racism, and lack of respect for authority. Here are a few statistical charts from available studies illustrating some of the violence-related drawbacks of television on our children. This is only one of many areas in which children are negatively affected.

The first chart illustrates the percent of programs containing violence at various viewing times.

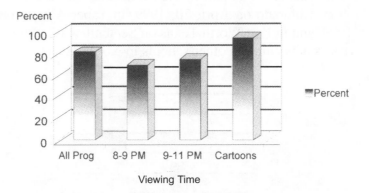

The second chart depicts the average number of violent acts per program hour. It is very clear from these two charts that the percent of violence and the average number of violent acts in cartoons are the highest compared to other programs. Cartoons are mainly directed at children. This means that children in this society are subjected to an immense amount of violence just by watching TV.

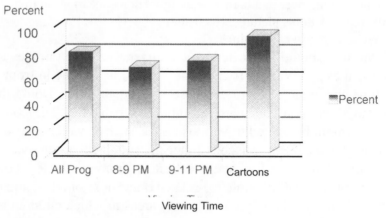

Viewing Time

The third chart shows the effect of violence at later stages in life for both male and female children. It is very clear that the effect on male children is much higher compared to the effect on female children. This could be part of the explanation of the massacres in Littleton, Colorado on April 20, 1999, in Taper Alberta on April 27, 1999, and in Fort Worth Texas on September 15, 1999, as well as what is happening in other schools in North America.

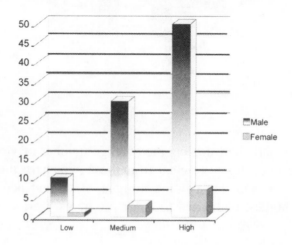

The studies also conclude that TV violence has specific effects on children, such as direct instruction and copying; disinhibition of aggressive and antisocial behavior; value shaping and cultivation effect; and divert attention from more important matters.

Due to the serious nature of the TV effects, we recommend that parents supervise and limit the viewing time that their children watch TV. Parents and children should select programs together to ensure that they are decent for viewing. Also, viewing time should not exceed an average of three hours a week. Healthy alternatives are available in forms of sports activities as well as Islamic videos. Parents are encouraged to visit the Sound Vision website for excellent tips on how to deal with children and TV.

ENVIRONMENT AS A SOURCE OF PRESSURE

In North America, Muslim children are faced with a tremendous amount of pressure. Parents have to realize that the environment that their children face is a completely different environment from that which they themselves faced when they were children. This must be taken into consideration in any *tarbiyah* plan. First of all, most parents were raised in a society where Muslims formed a majority, and as such, the Islamic behavior was accepted by the entire society. Also, positive enforcement of Islam was pervasive and constituted a great part of the support system for the children. For example, there was always something related to Islam and its basic principles in the various media sources (books, newspapers, radio, and television networks). There, Qur'anic recitation was always aired on radio and TV stations. The *adhan* (call to prayer) could be heard regularly everywhere the child turned. Mosques were spread in every corner of the city with scholars who were available to teach and answer questions almost 24 hours a day. Religious occassions were celebrated regularly. Parents were not shy to identify with Islam. On the whole, the atmosphere was very encouraging, conducive, peaceful, and supportive of anyone who chose to adhere to Islamic values and practice them (of course exceptions to this do exist, as in the harassment of dedicated Muslim groups by some governments).

Not only is this all-pervading positive enforcement absent from the life of Muslims in North American, but negative enforcement is at work, causing great strain. It is continuously being applied on Muslims or minorities in this land, severely affecting their children.

The following are some of the negative factors that Muslim children are subjected to in this society:

1. DAY-TO-DAY PEER PRESSURE AT SCHOOL: No doubt, peer pressure at school is the number one negative stress factor that Muslim or visible minority children are subjected to in the North American society. Considering the children's age, the school system and educational culture, the pressure mounts daily on children unless the parents interfere to prevent this build up.

In North America, the school system and the social structure of the classes are based on an effort to help the child be accepted by his or her classmates. Without doubt, a Muslim or minority child is at a disadvantage—unless he or she is outstanding in one area or another (i.e., athletics, academics, or art)—for the following reasons:

- language,
- dress code (especially for girls), and
- dietary habits and requirements.

Muslims have religious beliefs that often translate into actions that are contrary to the North American norms of dress, dietary habits, etc. These differences may be perceived as threatening by other classmates. Add to this, possible differences in skin color, language, and culture.

Parents play a significant role in eliminating or at least neutralizing this environmental pressure. It is covered in more detail later in this chapter.

2. RELIGIOUS HOLIDAYS' PRESSURE: Not permanent by nature, it takes place periodically during the celebration of certain religious holidays, such as Christmas and Easter. By far, Christmas time is the leading cause of pressure and stress for Muslim children. They are usually bombarded with questions from their peers such as "It's lots of fun. Why don't you have a decorated Christmas tree in your house?" "You mean to say you're not getting presents for the holiday season?!" "So why are you taking off for the Christmas holidays if you are not celebrating them?" "You don't believe in Jesus?" "You're not having a big turkey for Christmas dinner?" or "You're not writting a letter to Santa?" Similar questions are usually repeated during Easter. However, Christmas time is the worst for pressure due to commercialism and the lengthy period of its preparation.

Again, unless parents neutralize the social pressure on their children by helping them to understand the situation, these holidays have a serious negative impact on their upbringing.

3. PRESSURE DURING CERTAIN EVENTS: This type of pressure is usually started by media reporting of certain Islamic or Muslim world events. Stereotyping, double standards, bias against Islam are all part of the Western media's reporting of events related to Islam and Muslims; for example, *The Satanic Verses* affair, the Gulf War, the World Trade Center bombing, and the Oklahoma City bombing. The programs and analyses which followed the events tended to perpetuate a negative image of Muslims. In addition, due to the bias of media editors (with a few exceptions) against Muslims, Muslim responses to such events, are usually ignored and receive minimal media coverage (though there appears a slight improvement in media awareness these days). The absence of Muslim-owned television networks or cable companies does not help this problem. Thus, Muslims, and particularly Muslim children, feel the social pressure. The children's feeling of frustration and helplessness results in their desire to stay home from school.

Undoubtedly, the three pressures mentioned above have the worst influences on our children's behavior. Dealing with them represent our biggest challenge. But of course they are not the only pressures that Muslim children in North America face. Grouped according to age, the following is a more comprehensive list of problems faced by our children and their reactions from the resulting pressure:

Four to Five Years
- Refuses to go to school, cries, vomits, feels sick
- Stays alone in school, doesn't play with other children

Six to Eight Years
- Complains that other children don't play with him or her during recesses
- Complains that other kids hit him or her in the school
- Complains that some kids tease him or her and ridicule the type of food he or she eats at lunch
- Christmas-related problems
- Dress-related problems
- Problems related to the other gender

Nine to Eleven Years
- Make-up problems for girls
- Boy friend and girl friend issues
- Class parties toward the end of the year
- Invitation to mixed birthday parties
- The question of the WALKMAN, DISCMAN, CD player, MP3 player and cell phone
- Dress problems, specially in the beginning of summer when most girls start wearing shorts
- Swimming lessons for the class

High School Age
- School dances
- Gym uniforms
- Private parties, usually mixed and at private homes
- Friends
- Smoking and drugs
- Sex education

As parents, the above list of problems and sources of pressures should make us realize the magnitude of the challenge. Thus, through awareness we must strive to be prepared to meet the challenge of our children's upbringing.

PARENTS' ROLE IN ENSURING A PROPER ENVIRONMENT

To keep the *fitrah* (original nature) of a child, proper environment is a must. If society cannot provide such an environment, which is certainly the case in North American, parents' efforts have to be doubled or even tripled. First, they have to neutralize the negative stress factors; and, second, create a positive environment. With wisdom, hard work, and knowledge of Islam (with the help of Allah) parents can utilize the basic principles of *tarbiyah,* given in the previous chapter as well as the methods in chapter four, to motivate their children and minimize the impact of negative social influences. In some cases, parents can use the fact of being different to their children's advantage, raising their self-esteem. For example, knowing a second language gives children an advantage over their peers. Thus, parents can turn social forces to their children's advantage, creating the positive environment that makes their children strong individuals.

Certainly, parents are responsible for ensuring the presence of this environment. It is reported from Ibn 'Umar that the Prophet of Allah said:

> All of you are guardians and are responsible for your wards. The ruler is a guardian of his subjects and the man is a guardian for his family, the lady is a guardian and is responsible for her husband's house and his offspring; and so all of you are guardians and are responsible for your wards. (Bukhari)

SUPPORT SYSTEM

Islamic guidance provides support to its followers at four distinct levels. These levels range from the support given to an individual

through his or her own belief, to the support mutually practiced
between the individual and society. Parents can ensure a proper
environment for their children's upbringing by creating a support
system at the following levels:

Level 1: Support From Within

The starting point is linking the child to Allah through the ways
described in the previous chapter. Proper language and the use
of stories have a great effect. As the primary source of support,
children should grow up knowing the *Qur'an* and its message.

Individually, every Muslim is instructed to support himself or
herself through purifying the soul and following the right direction
as indicated in *Qur'an*:

$$\text{فَأَمَّا مَنْ طَغَى وَآثَرَ الْحَيَاةَ الدُّنْيَا فَإِنَّ الْجَحِيمَ هِيَ}$$

$$\text{الْمَأْوَى وَأَمَّا مَنْ خَافَ مَقَامَ رَبِّهِ وَنَهَى النَّفْسَ عَنِ الْهَوَى}$$

$$\text{فَإِنَّ الْجَنَّةَ هِيَ الْمَأْوَى}$$

As for the one who transgressed all bounds, and preferred the life
of this world, the abode will be hellfire. But as for the one who
feared to stand before his Lord, and restrained his soul from
lust and lower desires, the Garden will be his home. (79:37–41)

$$\text{وَنَفْسٍ وَمَا سَوَّاهَا فَأَلْهَمَهَا فُجُورَهَا وَتَقْوَاهَا قَدْ أَفْلَحَ مَنْ}$$

$$\text{زَكَّاهَا وَقَدْ خَابَ مَنْ دَسَّاهَا}$$

By the soul and proportion and order given to it, and its inspiration as to its wrong and its right; truly, the one that purifies it will
succeed, and the one that corrupts it will fail. (91:7–10)

$$\text{وَلَا تُلْقُوا بِأَيْدِيكُمْ إِلَى التَّهْلُكَةِ}$$

. . . And make not your own hands contribute to (your) destruc-
tion. (2:195)

At the same time a Muslim is asked to enjoy the goodness of this life without exceeding the limits, while he or she is seeking the pleasure of Allah:

وَابْتَغِ فِيمَا آتَاكَ اللَّهُ الدَّارَ الاخِرَةَ وَلَا تَنسَ نَصِيبَكَ مِنْ الدُّنْيَا وَأَحْسِنْ كَمَا أَحْسَنَ اللَّهُ إِلَيْكَ وَلَا تَبْغِ الْفَسَادَ فِي الارْضِ إِنَّ اللَّهَ لا يُحِبُّ الْمُفْسِدِينَ

But seek the abode of the Hereafter in that which Allah has given you, and neglect not your portion of the world: but do good, as Allah has been good to you, and seek not (occasions for) mischief in the land: for Allah loves not those who do mischief. (28:77)

وَكُلُوا وَاشْرَبُوا وَلَا تُسْرِفُوا

Eat and drink and waste not by excess. (7:31)

كُلُّ نَفْسٍ بِمَا كَسَبَتْ رَهِينَةٌ

Also Islam makes everyone responsible for his or her own deeds:

لَهَا مَا كَسَبَتْ وَعَلَيْهَا مَا اكْتَسَبَتْ

Every soul will be held in pledge for its deeds. (74:38)

Every soul gets every good that it earns, and suffers every ill that it earns. (2:286)

وَأَنْ لَيْسَ لِلانسَانِ إلا مَا سَعَى

That man can have nothing but what he strives for. (53:39)

The above teachings instill in the Muslim the sense of being responsible and make him or her an auditor of his or her own deeds. Devoted Muslims evaluate and assess their deeds on a regular basis to improve their performance as vicegerents of Allah on this earth. This is a great source of support for Muslims.

The above concepts work with children as well if they are intro-
duced in a very simple manner. Allocate time to review with your
children daily or weekly activities. Remind them that Allah loves
them because they believe in Him, and when Allah loves someone,
He supports that person at all levels and on every occassion. Recite
some of the Qur'anic verses which support what you say. For example, Allah says in the Qur'an:

إِنَّا لَنَنصُرُ رُسُلَنَا وَالَّذِينَ آمَنُوا فِي الْحَيَاةِ الدُّنْيَا وَيَوْمَ يَقُومُ الاشْهَادُ

We will, without doubt, help our messengers and those who
believe, (both) in this world's life and on the day when the witness will stand forth. (40:51)

اللَّهُ وَلِيُّ الَّذِينَ آمَنُوا

Allah is the supporter of those who believe. (2:257)

إِنَّ اللَّهَ مَعَ الَّذِينَ اتَّقَوْا وَالَّذِينَ هُمْ مُحْسِنُونَ

Allah is with those who are pious and those who practice *ihsan*.
(16:128)

It is also important to relate stories from the Prophet's biography
and Islamic history that demonstrate Allah's support for His Messenger and the Muslims during difficult times, such as: the Battle of
Badr, and the migration of the Prophet from Makkah to Madinah.
Teach your children that Allah is with them all the time. Train them
to ask Allah for whatever they need and to recite *du'as* for various
occasions, especially those that seek refuge in Allah such as:

I seek refuge in the perfect words of Allah from the evil ones of His
creation.

In the name of Allah, with whose name nothing hurts in the heavens
or earth.

وَهُوَ مَعَكُمْ أَيْنَ مَا كُنتُمْ

He is with you wherever you are. (57:4)

Prayers link children to Allah and make them feel secure wherever they are. It provides a great support system for the child from within.

Level 2: The Family Unit

The family unit is the second level of support that parents can provide for their children. The following are basic criteria for a successful family unit:

•   *Knowledge of Islam*

Islamic knowledge gives parents the tools and patience they need to bring up their children. From an Islamic perspective, the importance of knowledge cannot be overemphasized. Qur'anic verses and the practices of the Prophet illustrate this fact repeatedly. The first verse revealed to the Prophet Muhammad is a great proof of this:

$$ اقْرَأْ بِاسْمِ رَبِّكَ $$

Read in the name of your Lord. (96:1)

Another *surah* of the very early revelation emphasizes the tools of seeking knowledge:

$$ ن وَالْقَلَمِ وَمَا يَسْطُرُونَ $$

Nun. By the pen and by the (record) which (men) write. (68:1)

Also, the Qur'an makes a clear distinction between those who know and those who don't:

$$ قُلْ هَلْ يَسْتَوِي الَّذِينَ يَعْلَمُونَ وَالَّذِينَ لا يَعْلَمُونَ $$

. . . Say: are they equal, those who know and those who don't know. (39:9)

The Prophet is reported to have said:

Seeking knowledge is an obligation on every Muslim, male or female. (Ibn Majah and Baihaqi)

Also it is reported that he said:

... Allah, the angels, and the dwellers in the heavens and earth, even an ant in its hole and fish (in the depth of water) invoke blessings on one who teaches people goodness. (Tirmidhi)

In another hadith narrated by Anas the Prophet said:

One who goes out to search for knowledge is (devoted) to the cause of Allah till he returns. (Tirmidhi)

Also he is reported to have said:

He to whom Allah intends to show goodness, He gives him understanding of *din*. (Agreed upon)

In Islam, seeking knowledge is not a mere academic exercise or intellectual luxury. The Prophet teaches us that to be rewarded, one should use his or her knowledge properly (i.e., one should act upon what he or she knows).

The *Qur'an* and the practices of the Prophet provide ample examples illustrating the healthy parent-child relationship. They also provide parents with a clear understanding of the following concepts:

- Role and place of the human being in this universe and his purpose; thus providing clear goals and objectives of existence.
- Concepts of responsibility and accountability.
- Importance of *tarbiyah* and the great reward of parents who provide their children with proper Islamic *tarbiyah*.
- The great reward for those who teach right knowledge and who guide others to the straight path.

As such, knowledgeable parents who understand Islam properly and practice it in their daily life, will undoubtedly be in a much better position as a family unit to provide the support needed by their children and help their *tarbiyah* process. Setting an example and providing a role model is the highest level of support a family unit can give children.

You may say, "But I am not that type of parent." Let me assure you my dear reader that none of us were this type of parent when we had our first child. The good qualities required to provide the proper support to your children are not inherited. They come by training. You learn while you are raising your children. You accumulate knowledge and experience passing through stages of life. You have to work hard to achieve the skills required to be committed, dedicated, and supportive parents. As we said, these qualities can be acquired through training. The Prophet told us,

> . . . the one who exercises patience, Allah will give him patience. (Agreed upon)

and

> Knowledge is achieved by learning, and achieving forbearance comes only by practice. (Tabarani)

• An Attitude of Open Communication

Good, open communication with your children is a result of conferring regularly with them. You can begin as early as the second year of your child's life or even earlier. The key is effective listening or learning how to listen.

Our children need to communicate and be understood, particularly by their parents. So why is it then they won't talk to us? What can we do to get the communication flowing?

First and foremost, learn to listen effectively—be "active listeners." This means the following:

- LISTEN to both spoken and body messages. Less than 20 percent of what is communicated comes from words. We communicate more through tone of voice, eye contact, facial expressions, and body position. (Taping some family times together, with the permission of everyone involved, can be informative.)
- REFLECT upon what you believe your child is saying and feeling without judging or trying to solve his or her problem. Allow him or her to elaborate.

- CLARIFY whether your understanding is correct or whether you have misinterpreted? Are there important details that you have overlooked?
- EMPATHIZE by putting yourself in your child's position. It may help to try to recall a similar incident you have experienced. Tell your child you understand and care how he or she feels.

These four things may be enough. Remember, the primary need of children is to communicate and be understood. But if children ask for help in dealing with a particular situation, then try to *solve the problem* by asking what they think might help and if there is anything you can do. Be careful, don't impose your ideas on them, put it as suggestions, and give them the choice.

This sort of effective listening will not only ensure you really hear what your children are saying, it will signal to them that you can accept and understand all those other things they have wanted to share, and then the real communication begins. It is a great source of support.

Parents have to speak to their children on their own level. It is reported that the Prophet was like a child when he spoke to children, and like a youth when he spoke with youth. He shared their interests and spoke on their level. It is said:

Talk to people according to their level. Would you like them to deny the sayings of Allah and his Messenger?!

Sharing activities with your children is very important for their development. It enhances this communication channel and makes them feel at ease while communicating. More details on sharing activities with your child will come later.

- *Love and Tenderness*

Children should feel that their parents love them and value their correct development. Love and tenderness toward children have to be illustrated by parents on every occasion so that they feel that the home is the first place to turn to in case of problems and hardships. The open channel of communication described earlier is a great asset in such cases. Imagine children who cannot communicate with their parents, do not feel at ease communicating with them, and do not feel love and tenderness coming from them. Would they discuss their problems with their parents? Most probably not. They would rather talk to a teacher at school or to a close friend. If the teacher or friend have a different value system then there are further complications.

Support provided to children by the immediate family goes a long way to ensure a healthy environment for their upbringing. Without this support, it is very difficult to raise a child with the qualities we talked about in the first chapter of this book.

Below is an example of how a child can appreciate parental support. The following is a poem written by one of our daughters, thanking us for what we did for her.

A Thank You to My Parents

What would I do
without both of you,
Gently, but firmly
guiding me through?
Would I do drugs
until I was high?
Stay up late nights
in my bedroom and cry?
Would I kill?
Would I steal?
Would my heart be
too wounded to heal?
Would I laugh
when I hear
remarks which should
awaken fear?
Would I question
or even cared
if something
was fair?
Or would things be too blurred anyway?
What would I be like
without you guys
warning me, informing me,
opening my eyes?
Would I rebel and then fight
for something not right?
Or would I go along,
out of cowardice and fright?
Would I pretend to be cool,
knowing that I'm not,
When I've ruined my life
with hashish and pot?
Would I be confused,
Felt worthless and used,
To come back
for more substance abuse?

Or would I such pretend
so that, even if I hate them
with them I do blend?
Would I my secrets say
Though I know they would betray
because things are too blurred anyway?
I don't know what I'd be like
without the two of you.
But frankly, in all honesty
I hope I never do.
I know that with your guidance
I was blessed with Islam.
I know that I plan ahead
for a test I wouldn't cram.

I know that when I'm invited
to a party of the drug sort
There is no doubt,
it's clear in my mind
"No," I will retort!
And when I see my friends'
popularity, they stare and drool,
And do so many foolish things
to prove that they are cool,
I know that it's pathetic,
disgusting, and distasteful
And I know that to Allah
and to you two
I am grateful.

Level 3: Extended Family

For Muslims who were raised in Muslim countries before migrating to North America, the extended family provided a great source of support. Children who had arguments or little problems with their parents always found an aunt, an uncle, a grandpa, or a grandma to talk to. They cared about the children and provided the needed support. In fact, in some cases they even lived in the same big family house with them. There was always someone to speak to and find comfort in conferring with. Members of the extended family had the time to sit, talk, listen, discuss and do what it takes to keep the child-parent relationship sound. They saw it as part of their duty to build a strong Muslim family and hence a strong Muslim society.

Today in North America, Muslims do not have the luxury of the extended family. In most cases, both parents work and spend most of their time outside the house. As a result, the children seem lost. Children's needs are not met because parents have no time for them. Can parents do something to fill in for the absence of the extended family? Sure they can. The best way, which we found through experimentation, is to form a "buddy" system with one or two other families. In this system, the children feel they are part of the families with which you have created a bond of friendship. It is the substitute for the extended family. If you are busy or if you have a problem communicating with your children, they can share their concerns with other families. Here are some tips in selecting such families:

- They should share the same understanding of Islam as a complete and comprehensive way of life;
- They should be striving, or at least willing to strive, to practice this understanding; and
- Of course they should have children around the same age as your children.

One way of finding such families is through Islamic center and mosque activities. If you, as a family, regularly participate in study circles taking place in your Islamic center or attend lessons given by the Imam or a learned person in the center, there is a high possibility that you will meet such families. If there is no study circle in your mosque, start one. Center the activities around family concerns. Organize it well and make it attractive. If there is no one in your community to lead a study circle, pick authentic books to study. There is nothing wrong with not knowing the answer to a question and then researching it later.

Cultivate relations with your "buddy" families through regular activities like group picnics, swimming classes for ladies and girls, other sports events, joint Islamic days and seminars, or camps.

OTHER SUPPORT MECHANISMS

Parents and community members can play a great role in neutralizing the effects of a negative environment on their children, especially from the public schools. Here are some ideas for you to consider:

- *Visit the public school.* These visits should be done by either parents or concerned members of the community. The purpose of these visits would be to:

- in a friendly way, explain to non-Muslim children why Muslim children do what they do and say what they say, why they don't celebrate Christmas, what Muslim children celebrate, what Ramadan is, and what is *'Id*.

- make school officials aware of Muslim children's needs, such as having a quite place for *zuhr* prayer, or dietary needs during school sponsored lunches.

- participate with their children in classroom "show and tell" activity, particularly before Islamic events such as Ramadan and *'Id*s.

- arrange information displays about Islam in an open house fashion in the school gym or corridors (of course this has to be done in coordination with school officials).

- *Volunteer time for school activities.* Parents should volunteer their time to help with school activities: supervising field trips, helping in serving school lunch, and participating in sporting activities. This spirit of cooperation and service leaves a good impression with school officials and makes them open-minded and understanding to Muslim children's needs. At the same time it supports Muslim children who see their parents as part of the school. Their peers will meet you and know you as helpful and nice people. They will see you in real life—acting, helping, caring, and eating with them. They will see that your children are no different from them except maybe for the type and form of dress. In addition, the interaction between you and the parents of your children's peers is very important to your children. All in all, this exercise provides a great deal of support and helps in neutralizing most of the negative forces coming from public school.

- *Send notes to school.* Parents should send detailed notes with their children to the school officials about upcoming Islamic events and request that the school announce them on the PA system at the morning assembly. As a result non-Muslim children will know about these events and wouldn't be surprised when they see Muslim children fasting in Ramadan, for example.

- *Organize camps for Muslim youth.* Parents as well as concerned community members should make sure that useful activities such as camps are organized for the children, especially during Christmas vacation and summer. The camp program should include activities that attract the children. Sports activities, games, sketches, as well as contests are very effective ways of teaching. Of course teaching Qur'anic recitation and *sirah* of the Prophet should be part of any camp program.

- *Form boys and girls clubs.* The idea of a boys only club or a girls only club is very appealing to young Muslims. It can be done either in the Islamic center, if it has a multipurpose hall, or better still, at a community center that has sports facilities. It could be done on a weekly basis or bi-weekly. Activities such as sports, games, crafts, art work, visits to museums and historical places within the city or in a close-by city are common for this type of arrangement. Visiting other Muslim groups in adjacent cities, as well as cooking demonstrations could be very attractive for the children. These activities help create a strong bond among Muslim children and leaves good memories.

- *Form an Islamic* nashīd *(singing) group.* This is a very good idea to occupy the time of those children who enjoy singing and being members of choir groups. It could be held for two hours twice a week or more. A community member who has some experience in this area has to be responsible for such an activity, and he or she would have to be aided by parents. It is useful to group the participants according to their age. Make sure that the songs are decent, easy to learn and educational. Some songs that cover the *sirah* of the Prophet could also be used. Allow the children to perform in community celebrations and gatherings. This will have a great impact on the children's self-esteem and make them feel that they are contributing to the community's well-being. Again, these types of activities go a long way in providing support to our young Muslims.

- *Hold overnight parties.* This is another source of support parents can provide to their children. Sleepover parties organized by the children with other Muslim children and supervised by parents is lots of fun for them and helps create a strong bond of friendship between them. It also has the benefit of making the children feel that they are equal with their peers. They will have something to talk about next day in the school.

- *Organize sports activities.* Sports activities provide a healthy environment for children to build good relationships with other children. It also provides a wonderful platform for parents and children to create a strong bond. Parents should try to organize regular tournaments in various sporting activities, such as soccer and basketball. It may be a good idea to invite young Muslims from nearby cities to have a field day in your city. Regular sports activities are very healthy and occupy the children's time in a useful way. These activities should be used by adults to teach children various moral values and lessons of teamwork and cooperation.

Fathers, especially, should participate with their male children in sports activities organized by the public school, or within the community. They should drive them to games, and be there to give them support.

All of the above ideas have been tried in one community or another and have proved to be successful in providing great support to Muslim children. Parents can come up with other useful ideas that suit the special situation of their children. But it is important to realize that to implement these ideas parents have to work hard and sacrifice their time. You may have to spend time in organizational meetings and driving your children to these activities. Occasionally, you will have to make your house available for some of these sleepovers. Yes, it may take part of your time and effort, but it will be worth it.

Summary

In this chapter, we discussed various aspects related to the environment. The importance of the environment was pointed out with the help of prophet Muhammad's sayings. Various circles of the environment were identified. The effects of society, especially that of TV, on children was highlighted using several charts covering violence. The environment as a source of pressure was discussed with the specific mention of various types of pressures Muslim children are subjected to in the North American environment. Among these are day-to-day peer pressure, religious holiday pressures, and pressures accompanying certain events. A list of problems faced by Muslim children attending the public school system was presented. The parent's role in ensuring a proper environment for their children was discussed in detail. Recommended support mechanisms were suggested for parents such as support from within, unit family support, extended family support as well as other support mechanisms including school visits, volunteering time for school activities, Muslim youth camps, boys and girls clubs, and sports activities.

CHAPTER 4

WAYS AND MEANS OF *TARBIYAH*

In his book, *The Methodology of Islamic Tarbiyah,* Dr. Muhammad Qutb lists the following methods of *tarbiyah*:

- leadership and example (role model),
- exhortation, (warning or gentle advice),
- punishment and discipline,
- stories,
- directing and exerting energy,
- time utilization,
- habituation (*tarbiyah* by habits), and
- *tarbiyah* by events.

He maintains that all the methods of upbringing that are available to Muslims, haven't been utilized fully by them. Each method affects a different facet of the individual, so the use of all of them would result in an individual undergoing a complete *tarbiyah*. In this chapter, with the help of Dr. Qutb's writings, we discuss the details of each method and how to use it in the North American context.

UPBRINGING BY LEADERSHIP

Teaching *tarbiyah* by leadership is the most effective method and the closest one to success. It is easy to create a book about upbringing. It is easy to imagine an agenda, even if it still needs improvement in proficiency and unity. Yet the agenda remains simply ink on paper, suspended in space until it is practiced in everyday life, until it becomes an individual interpreting—by his actions, emotions, and thoughts—its meaning. Only then does the agenda become a reality, a movement, an event in history.

When Allah made the heavenly and miraculous agenda, He knew that there would be humans. In His wisdom He knew that the human heart would carry out His agenda and transform it into reality, so that mankind would know that it is the truth and then follow it. There had to be a leader to carry the message, there had to be a role model. For this, Allah sent the Prophet Muhammad:

لَقَدْ كَانَ لَكُمْ فِي رَسُولِ اللَّهِ أُسْوَةٌ حَسَنَةٌ

Verily in the messenger of Allah you have a good example. (33:21)

In the personality of the Prophet, He put the complete picture of the Islamic model—alive and eternal.

When 'A'ishah was asked about the character of the Prophet, she answered,

His character was the *Qur'an*. (Muslim)

Imagine, such an interesting, accurate, concise, and complete answer: "His character was the (reflection of) *Qur'an*!" He was a living interpretation of the *Qur'an*—its realities and directions. Therefore he was, just like the *Qur'an*, a great power in existence. A power of Allah's making, full in every aspect of the law; and in the law, a complete power. And so the sky and earth come together in the most amazing meeting creation has ever seen. It is no wonder that his birth was the birth of light.

Finally, science has realized that matter is a statement of energy and that energy can change into a glow. Finally, it has come to realize also that the human soul, with its God-given intuition is a power, and that the human soul power becomes a glow, becomes a light.

Yet, the ultimate realization of man's potential and power is the Prophet Muhammad. He was power from the transparent light that Allah sent to light up the path for people on earth,

يَاأَيُّهَا النَّبِيُّ إِنَّا أَرْسَلْنَاكَ شَـاهِدًا وَمُبَشِّرًا وَنَذِيرًا(٤٥)وَدَاعِيًا إِلَى اللَّـهِ بِإِذْنِهِ وَسِرَاجًا مُنِيرًا

O Prophet! Lo! We have sent you as a witness and a bringer of good tidings and a warner. And as a summoner unto Allah by His permission, and as a lamp that gives light. (33:45–46)

And this light overflowed in the hearts of the created beings, and it uncovered the paths for people and they passed along them, peaceful and noble.

The light of guidance dazzled each individual soul, and so hung onto it and loved it in a way no one has ever loved anyone in the world. No one has ever received the love that the Prophet Muhammad received, even from his enemies, the enemies of Allah's religion. The battle between the truth and falsehood took place as it naturally would, and naturally the truth won. So false-hood, which had obscured the light from mankind, was removed. This light remained in the Prophet Muhammad, glowing radiantly: "light upon light," as Allah wanted it, leading people to the straight path throughout the centuries and tying their hearts to Allah.

Muhammad is one of the miracles of all the miracles found in the creation, coming from Allah, a miracle just like Allah's verses—great and glorious . . . with no limits!

The Prophet Muhammad is, as it were, many individuals rolled into one. Each facet of his blessed character is so complete that if he only possessed one character trait he would be a complete and perfect individual. But all individuals are joined together in him—all complete—forming a vast horizon, synchronized to form a uni-fied field of balance and harmony. He is a pure and transparent soul equal and more in spirituality to Jesus, who "specialized" in spiri-tuality.

The Prophet Muhammad had a liveliness and an emanating power that reached every person he met, as if he focused only on emanating this power. He solved issues with all his effort. He fought against evil like a storm that couldn't be stopped. 'Ali ibn Abi Talib said about him:

> The bravest one of us was the closest one to the Prophet during battle. He could have been enjoying all the riches and beauties of life, as if he were someone who had the time and capacity to enjoy such things. He greeted people with peace, warmth, and cordiality. If he was happy and content, it was so manifested in him that his friends could see it in his face and eyes. And if he was angry or upset, it too would be so manifested on his face that he would be perspiring. So was inner strength and emotion alive in him in every way and circumstance.

He was also a man of policy, who brought up a nation of scattered tribes into an enormous, strong force incomparable to anything else in history. This strong force issued from his strength, intellect, soul, effort, and emotions would keep lives fully busy.

He was a warrior who planned and implemented, who led soldiers, who fought and won. He was perfected in this role too, as though "specializing" in it, and nothing could distract him from his mission.

He was a husband, a father, and a leader of a family. As a family, they made many sacrifices, not only of wealth, but of their souls, their intellects, their emotions, their very beings. To his family too, he was fully dedicated, he was a "specialist." Nothing could distract him from that either.

He was a relative, a friend, and a companion to all people. Their worries were his worries. Their emotions were his emotions. He did not forget them. He would return to visit them, comfort them, and help them through any of their problems. He gave from his feelings, his wisdom, and his time, so that he was completely dedicated to the well-being of his people.

He was a worshipper completely inclined to his Lord. He was a man dedicated to his spiritual well-being, as if it and only it mattered, with nothing linking him to the present world, no worries or desires to distract him from his worship.

And with all this, he was the leader of the most phenomenal message ever sent to humanity. This message gave humanity its full purpose in life. It touched and affected every person in every aspect of his or her life.

All these personal qualities were combined into one person. They were all coordinated and balanced, and they all received their full share to reach their ultimate potential. No quality failed or dominated because the individual who carried them, Muhammad, the Prophet of Allah, was supported by Allah's power—a power far beyond our imagination.

This is the Prophet Muhammad, the son of Abd Allah, the light which awed and shone upon all beings. People loved him, admired him, and followed him.

It is God's wisdom to send a being so balanced and whole, just as He sent the *Qur'an*. For the Prophet Muhammad himself was a sign, directly proportional to the *Qur'an*. His personality, his actions, his beliefs were the *Qur'an*.

He was also a practical model and an extraordinary leader of people. For he was not a fictional character in a book; he was a living person, with the same needs, desires, and problems as others. His companions were able to become familiar with him and, therefore, to empathize with him, learn from him, and follow him. They were able to grasp his teachings, for he was not a dream nor a fantasy.

Therefore, he was the greatest, most complete model ever given to humanity. However, even before he spoke the words of God, his manner of speaking and emphasizing was what made people believe in him. In His way, Allah nurtured this *ummah* (community of believers) of Muhammad, to which He refers in the *Qur'an*:

$$كُنْتُمْ خَيْرَ أُمَّةٍ أُخْرِجَتْ لِلنَّاسِ تَأْمُرُونَ بِالْمَعْرُوفِ وَتَنْهَوْنَ عَـنْ الْمُنْكَرِ$$
$$وَتُؤْمِنُونَ بِاللَّهِ$$

You are the best *ummah* given to mankind: You enjoin what is good and forbid what is evil and you believe in Allah. (3:110)

Allah has also said about this *ummah:*

لَقَدْ مَنَّ اللَّهُ عَلَى الْمُؤْمِنِينَ إِذْ بَعَثَ فِيهِمْ رَسُولًا مِنْ أَنْفُسِهِمْ يَتْلُوا عَلَيْهِمْ آيَاتِهِ وَيُزَكِّيهِمْ وَيُعَلِّمُهُمُ الْكِتَابَ وَالْحِكْمَةَ وَإِنْ كَانُوا مِنْ قَبْلُ لَفِي ضَلَالٍ مُبِينٍ

Allah has been kind to the believers for He has sent from among them a messenger to read to them His signs, to purify them and to teach them the Book and wisdom. Verily, before this they had gone astray. (3:164)

This leadership will last as long as the heavens and the earth.

The personality of the Prophet isn't a sign for one era, generation, nation, school of thought, or region; it is a universal sign, for all people and all generations without exception:

وَمَا أَرْسَلْنَاكَ إِلَّا رَحْمَةً لِلْعَالَمِينَ

We have only sent you as a mercy for all creatures. (21:107)

وَمَا أَرْسَلْنَاكَ إِلَّا كَافَّةً لِلنَّاسِ بَشِيرًا وَنَذِيرًا

We have only sent you as a bringer of good tidings and a warner to all people. (34:28)

He is for the whole universe, all people in all times and places, as an example that never disappears or deteriorates. For he is alive now just as he was alive on the Arabian peninsula fourteen hundred years ago. He has not changed or diminished, just as the sun and physical laws of the universe have not changed or diminished. When the story of his life is read, it touches people and it moves them at their core like no other thing can ever move them.

Of course, it is natural that those who witnessed the Prophet Muhammad and received light directly from him, received the full charging of their souls, hearts, thoughts, and feelings. So they soared, creating some of the most phenomenal achievements of history, just as does concentrated atomic energy soar, creating amazing things.

The live power that came through the Prophet was fully absorbed by those who opened themselves and their feelings to it. It overflowed from them, alive and strong. Today, its reality cannot be denied.

How many a small, obscure nation has survived for generations inspired by its local "hero." The more the hero gains acceptance, the more encompassing the influence of his life becomes, the greater is his presence among the people. By the same token, wouldn't he who invites the earth to the heavens achieve an even higher degree? After all, his message is the sign that encompasses the essence of life.

Allah sent the Prophet Muhammad to every human being and to all things in the world. The Prophet knew best the method of His message, the truth of the Creator, the Gentle, the Amiable, the All-knowing. Allah made the Prophet the continuing leader and example for humanity, so that we could see a live translation of the *Qur'an* in his personality; so that we could believe in this religion and witness that Islam can be achieved in this life.

Islam's leading example is the personality of its prophet, for it is an example that is renewable throughout the passage of generations and relevant to people's natures. However, Islam does not offer this example simply so that one may be amazed by it without learning and acting from it. Islam offers the example of the Prophet so that people may strive to achieve his qualities within themselves, according to their ability. In this manner, the Prophet's example doesn't become one that people adore but do not understand; it is a goal that people aim for and remain personally in touch with.

Islam deems leadership by example to be the best method of upbringing. It bases its entire method of upbringing on this foundation. First, children must have an example of leadership in their own families and in their parents, so that they may grow up with an Islamic foundation. Second, people must have an example of leadership in their society to imprint in them Islamic values and ethics and thus raise generations of good believers. And there must be an example for the whole society in their leader, or governor who fulfills good works so others can follow him. And the ultimate example for all is the Prophet of Islam.

Children learn what they see, not what they hear—eyes remember actions, and brains register pictures.

Dr. Qutb continues:

> The child who witnesses his father lying cannot learn to be truthful. The child whose father is harsh and tough with him cannot learn to be merciful and cooperative. The child who sees his mother cheating cannot learn to be honest . . .

The family is the immediate circle of environment and has the greatest impact on a child's development. As such, it is very important that the family provides a good example. Parents are responsible, nobody else, to provide a role model for their children. In a society full of very strange role models, you cannot afford not to provide this good example for your child. If you, as a parent don't do it, if you as a parent don't provide the clean Islamic model for your child at home, he or she will find it outside, maybe among the basketball stars or actors, such as Charles Barkley or Madonna. Before you can give *tarbiyah* to your children, evaluate your values, your actions, and your habits. See what is Islamic and what is not. Providing *tarbiyah* may take a great deal of effort and a great deal of patience and hard work, but it is a great investment for you yourself and the generations you want to raise. Check "self-search" in the first chapter of this book. Knowing ourselves is achievable as long as our motives are purely to please Allah by being better Muslims and providing better examples for our children. Our sources of knowledge should be the *Qur'an* and the *sirah*, the *Sunnah*, of the Prophet—after all, we want to provide the right example for our children and the best example is the Prophet Muhammad.

The following are some areas where parents can set the right example for their children and where they will follow, God willing:

- Supervised, limited TV viewing;
- Observing regular prayer at home, as a family;
- Being active in Islamic work and giving for the sake of Allah;

- Cooperation;
- Sharing and helping others; and
- Being humble.

Here is how our oldest daughter (20 years at the time of writing) views the importance of having a role model.

Role modeling is one of the most effective ways of raising children, for most people will follow in the footsteps of their parents. There are certain key things in the way my parents presented themselves as role models that helped me become who I am today. First, to them, being a role model did not mean that all my sisters and I had to do everything they did, the way they did them. They knew that when we decided to do something, it should be because we were convinced it was for the best. They did this by explaining to us the reasoning behind anything we did and, most importantly, by doing it themselves. The best proof of something's effectiveness is seeing a live example of it. Second, they agreed on the example they wanted to present. This is a crucial point, for even though they are two separate people, as a role model they have to present one picture. Finally, having a role model at home helped me feel secure that I did not have to search for the truth elsewhere, and it is this peace of mind that can never be replaced by anything else.

Here is how our 14 year-old sees the importance of a role model:

One of the many things I've learned from having two wonderful role models is that one should do one's best in all things. My parents are both very hardworking and I have never seen them give less than their best effort in a job or task. They are actively involved with Muslim communities in North America at various levels. My father has a very demanding job. In short, they are very busy. However, as I said, they are always available to help and do their best in any activities they are involved in. When people tell you to work hard, but don't work hard themselves, they're telling you "Do as I say, don't do as I do." This isn't a very effective way to get people to follow on the right path. By doing what you want others to do, you get a better response. I think this is why my sisters and I have all grown up to be hardworking students. Without our parents as role models we wouldn't have had the inspiration.

Upbringing by Exhortation, Admonition, and Gentle Advice

Dr. Qutb indicates that exhortation, admonition and gentle advice alone without good example cannot provide a good means of *tarbiyah*. When the good example is present and clear, exhortation can be used to complement it, then it proves to have a great impact on human soul. *Qur'an* used exhortation in so many occasions such as in the following verses:

وَاعْبُدُوا اللَّهَ وَلا تُشْرِكُوا بِهِ شَيْئًا وَبِالْوَالِدَيْنِ إِحْسَانًا وَبِـذِي الْقُرْبَى وَالْيَتَامَى وَالْمَسَاكِينِ وَالْجَارِ ذِي الْقُرْبَى وَالْجَارِ الْجُنُبِ وَالصَّاحِبِ بِالْجَنْبِ وَابْنِ السَّبِيلِ وَمَا مَلَكَتْ أَيْمَانُكُمْ إِنَّ اللَّهَ لا يُحِبُّ مَنْ كَانَ مُخْتَالا فَخُورًا

Serve Allah, and join not any partners with Him; and do good to parents, kinsfolk, orphans, those in need, neighbors who are of kin, neighbors who are strangers, the companion by your side, the wayfarer (you meet) and what your right hands possess: For Allah loves not the arrogant, the vainglorious. (4:36)

إِنَّ اللَّهَ يَأْمُرُكُمْ أَنْ تُؤَدُّوا الامَانَاتِ إِلَى أَهْلِهَا وَإِذَا حَكَمْتُمْ بَيْنَ النَّاسِ أَنْ تَحْكُمُوا بِالْعَدْلِ إِنَّ اللَّهَ نِعِمَّا يَعِظُكُمْ بِهِ إِنَّ اللَّهَ كَانَ سَمِيعًا بَصِيرًا

Allah does comand you to render back your trusts to those to whom they are due; and when you judge between people that you judge with justice: Verily how excellent is the teaching which He gives you! For Allah is He who hears and sees all things. (4:58)

وَإِذْ قَالَ لُقْمَانُ لابْنِهِ وَهُوَ يَعِظُهُ يَابُنَيَّ لا تُشْرِكْ بِاللَّهِ إِنَّ الشِّرْكَ لَظُلْمٌ عَظِيمٌ(١٣) وَوَصَّيْنَا الانسَانَ بِوَالِدَيْهِ حَمَلَتْهُ أُمُّهُ وَهْنًا عَلَى وَهْنٍ وَفِصَالُهُ فِي عَامَيْنِ أَنْ اشْكُرْ لِي وَلِوَالِدَيْكَ إِلَيَّ الْمَصِيرُ(١٤) وَإِنْ جَاهَدَاكَ عَلَى

أَنْ تُشْرِكَ بِي مَا لَيْسَ لَكَ بِهِ عِلْمٌ فَـلا تُطِعْهُمَا وَصَاحِبْهُمَا فِي الدُّنْيَا
مَعْرُوفًا وَاتَّبِعْ سَبِيلَ مَنْ أَنَابَ إِلَيَّ ثُمَّ إِلَيَّ مَرْجِعُكُمْ فَأُنَبِّئُكُمْ بِمَا كُنْتُمْ
تَعْمَلُونَ(١٥) يَابُنَيَّ إِنَّهَا إِنْ تَكُنْ مِثْقَالَ حَبَّةٍ مِنْ خَرْدَلٍ فَتَكُنْ فِي
صَخْرَةٍ أَوْ فِي السَّمَاوَاتِ أَوْ فِي الارْضِ يَـأْتِ بِهَا اللَّهُ إِنَّ اللَّهَ لَطِيفٌ
خَبِيرٌ(١٦) يَابُنَيَّ أَقِمِ الصَّلاةَ وَأْمُرْ بِالْمَعْرُوفِ وَانْهَ عَـنِ الْمُنكَرِ وَاصْبِرْ
عَلَى مَا أَصَابَكَ إِنَّ ذَلِكَ مِنْ عَزْمِ الامُورِ(١٧) وَلا تُصَعِّرْ خَـدَّكَ لِلنَّاسِ
وَلا تَمْشِ فِي الارْضِ مَرَحًا إِنَّ اللَّهَ لا يُحِبُّ كُـلَّ مُخْتَـالٍ فَخُورٍ(١٨)
وَاقْصِدْ فِي مَشْيِكَ وَاغْضُضْ مِنْ صَوْتِكَ إِنَّ أَنكَرَ الاصْـوَاتِ لَصَوْتُ
الْحَمِيرِ(١٩)

Behold, Luqman said to his son admonishing him, O my son!
Join not in worship (others) with Allah, for false worship is
indeed the highest wrongdoing. And We have enjoined on man
(to be good) to his parents: In travail upon travail did his mother
bear him. And in two years was his weaning: (Hear the com-
mand), Show gratitude to Me and to your parents. To Me is (your
final) goal. But if they strive to make you join in worship with Me
things of which you have no knowledge, obey them not: yet bear
them company in this life with justice (and consideration), and
follow the way of those who turn to Me. In the end, the return of
you all is to Me, and I will tell you all that you did. O my son!
(said Luqman), If there be (but) the weight of a mustard seed and
it were (hidden) in a rock, or (anywhere) in the heavens or on
earth, Allah will bring it forth, for Allah is Subtle and Aware. O
my son! Establish regular prayer, enjoin what is just, and forbid
what is wrong, and bear with patient constancy whatever befalls
you, for this is firmness (of purpose) in (the conduct of) affairs.
And swell not your cheek (for pride) at men. Nor walk in insolence upon the earth, for Allah loves not any arrogant boaster.
And be moderate in your pace, and lower your voice; for the
harshest of sounds without doubt is the braying of the donkey.
(31:13–19)

لا تَجْعَلْ مَعَ اللَّهِ إِلَهًا آخَرَ فَتَقْعُدَ مَذْمُومًا مَخْـذُولا(٢٢) وَقَضَى رَبُّكَ
أَلا تَعْبُدُوا إِلا إِيَّاهُ وَبِالْوَالِدَيْنِ إِحْسَانًا إِمَّا يَبْلُغَنَّ عِنْدَكَ الْكِبَرَ أَحَدُهُمَا أَوْ
كِلاهُمَا فَلا تَقُلْ لَهُمَا أُفٍّ وَلا تَنْهَرْهُمَا وَقُلْ لَهُمَا قَوْلا كَرِيمًا(٢٣)
وَاخْفِضْ لَهُمَا جَنَاحَ الذُّلِّ مِنَ الرَّحْمَةِ وَقُلْ رَبِّ ارْحَمْهُمَا كَمَا رَبَّيَانِي
صَغِيرًا(٢٤) رَبُّكُمْ أَعْلَمُ بِمَا فِي نُفُوسِكُمْ إِنْ تَكُونُوا صَالِحِينَ فَإِنَّهُ كَانَ
لِلأَوَّابِينَ غَفُورًا(٢٥) وَآتِ ذَا الْقُرْبَى حَقَّهُ وَالْمِسْكِينَ وَابْنَ السَّبِيلِ وَلا
تُبَذِّرْ تَبْذِيرًا(٢٦) إِنَّ الْمُبَذِّرِينَ كَانُوا إِخْوَانَ الشَّيَاطِينِ وَكَـانَ الشَّيْطَانُ
لِرَبِّهِ كَفُورًا(٢٧) وَإِمَّا تُعْرِضَنَّ عَنْهُمُ ابْتِغَاءَ رَحْمَةٍ مِنْ رَبِّكَ تَرْجُوهَا
فَقُلْ لَهُمْ قَوْلا مَيْسُورًا(٢٨) وَلا تَجْعَلْ يَدَكَ مَغْلُولَةً إِلَى عُنُقِكَ وَلا
تَبْسُطْهَا كُلَّ الْبَسْطِ فَتَقْعُدَ مَلُومًا مَحْسُورًا(٢٩) إِنَّ رَبَّكَ يَبْسُطُ الـرِّزْقَ
لِمَنْ يَشَاءُ وَيَقْدِرُ إِنَّهُ كَانَ بِعِبَادِهِ خَبِيرًا بَصِيرًا(٣٠) وَلا تَقْتُلُوا أَوْلادَكُمْ
خَشْيَةَ إِمْلاقٍ نَحْنُ نَرْزُقُهُمْ وَإِيَّاكُمْ إِنَّ قَتْلَهُمْ كَانَ خِطْئًا كَبِيرًا(٣١) وَلا
تَقْرَبُوا الزِّنَى إِنَّهُ كَانَ فَاحِشَةً وَسَاءَ سَبِيلا(٣٢) وَلا تَقْتُلُوا النَّفْـسَ الَّتِي
حَرَّمَ اللَّهُ إِلا بِالْحَقِّ وَمَنْ قُتِلَ مَظْلُومًا فَقَدْ جَعَلْنَا لِوَلِيِّهِ سُلْطَانًا فَلا
يُسْرِفْ فِي الْقَتْلِ إِنَّهُ كَانَ مَنْصُورًا(٣٣) وَلا تَقْرَبُوا مَالَ الْيَتِيمِ إِلا بِالَّتِي
هِيَ أَحْسَنُ حَتَّى يَبْلُغَ أَشُدَّهُ وَأَوْفُوا بِالْعَهْدِ إِنَّ الْعَهْدَ كَانَ مَسْئُولا(٣٤)
وَأَوْفُوا الْكَيْلَ إِذَا كِلْتُمْ وَزِنُوا بِالْقِسْطَاسِ الْمُسْتَقِيمِ ذَلِكَ خَيْرٌ وَأَحْسَنُ
تَأْوِيلا(٣٥) وَلا تَقْفُ مَا لَيْسَ لَكَ بِهِ عِلْمٌ إِنَّ السَّمْعَ وَالْبَصَرَ وَالْفُؤَادَ
كُلُّ أُولَئِكَ كَانَ عَنْهُ مَسْئُولا(٣٦) وَلا تَمْشِ فِي الأرْضِ مَرَحًا إِنَّكَ لَنْ
تَخْرِقَ الأرْضَ وَلَنْ تَبْلُغَ الْجِبَالَ طُولا(٣٧) كُلُّ ذَلِكَ كَـانَ سَيِّئُهُ عِنْدَ
رَبِّكَ مَكْرُوهًا (٣٨)

Take not with Allah another god; or you (O man!) will sit in disgrace and destitution. Your Lord has decreed that you worship none but Him, and that you be kind to parents. Whether one or both of them attain old age in your life, say not to them a word of contempt, nor repel them but address them in terms of honor. And, out of kindness, lower to them the wing of humility, and say: My Lord bestow on them Your mercy ever as they cherished me in childhood. Your Lord knows best what is in your hearts: If you do deeds of righteousness. Verily, He is Most-Forgiving to those who turn to Him again and again (in true penitence). And render to the kindred their due rights, as (also) to those in want, and to the wayfarer. But squander not (your wealth) in the manner of a spendthrift. Verily, spendthrifts are brothers of the satans. And the Satan is to his Lord (Himself) ungrateful. And even if you were to turn away from them in pursuit of the mercy from your Lord which you do expect, yet speak to them a word of easy kindness. Make not your hand tied to your neck, nor stretch it forth to its utmost reach, so that you become blame-worthy and destitute. Verily, your Lord provides sustenance in abundance for whom He pleases, and He straiten it for He knows and regards all His servants. Kill not your children for fear of want: We shall provide sustenance for them as well as for you. Verily, the killing of them is a great sin. Nor come nigh to adultery, for it is an indecent (deed) and an evil way, nor take life—which Allah has made sacred—except for just cause. And if anyone is slain wrongfully, we have given his heir authority (to demand compensation or to forgive), but let him not exceed bounds in the matter of taking life, for he is helped (by the Law). Come not near to the orphan's property except to improve it, until he attains the age of full strength; and fulfil (every) covenant, for (every) covenant will be enquired into (on the Day of Reckoning). Give full measure when you measure, and weigh with a balance that is correct; that is better and fairer in the final determination. And pursue not that of which you have no knowledge; for surely the hearing, the sight, the heart—all of those shall be questioned. Walk not on the earth with insolence, for you cannot rend the earth asunder or reach the mountains in height. The evil of all such things is hateful in the sight of your Lord. (17:22–38)

As a matter of fact, the *Qur'an* itself has been described as an "exhortation." Allah says about the *Qur'an*:

$$\text{هَذَا بَيَانٌ لِلنَّاسِ وَهُدًى وَمَوْعِظَةٌ لِلْمُتَّقِينَ}$$

This is a clear evidence for people, a guidance and an admonition for those who have *taqwa*. (3:138)

The following is an example in which admonition, along with a role model, played an important part in helping one of our daughters make a critical decision.

A decision every Muslim girl has to face, whether she lives in Nebraska, Makkah, or Japan: The decision to wear the *hijab*.

I just happened to be living in Ottawa, Canada, when I was faced with it. At the time I was a fourth grade student enjoying the freedom of a long teachers strike. While they walked the picket lines, I played in the backyard with my sisters and brainstormed over my list of *'Id* presents. Yes, *'Id* was coming up and my teachers were on strike. How wonderful! There'll be so much time to decorate the house, bake the goodies, and pick the new outfits!

So when I had to choose whether or not I would wear *hijab*, I was surrounded by Muslim friends and themes. So I decided that I was prepared to wear *hijab* and meet my public school friends at the beginning of the next school year. (The expectation was that the strike would go on for the rest of this year and we would return to school next year.)

Then, to my dismay, one night before I went to sleep my sister told me that the strike was over.

"Over! No! No! No! No! That can't be! The strike's not over until next year! What am I going to do?"

I put on my prayer clothes and prayed *isha'*. Though I said every word of *Surat al Fatiha* and did every *rak'ah* and every *sajdah*, my mind was not understanding the actions or the beautiful words. After the prayer, I went to the stairway railing where I stood calling my mother. She had visitors over that night and my father and her were sitting with them in the livingroom. I don't know how long I actually stood at the railing and whined for my mom, but it felt like forever. Finally, when she came, she found me weeping on my bed still in my prayer clothes. "Mama," I squeaked, " the strike is over."

"Yes I know, Sweetie." my mother said, squeezing my hand.

"What am I going to do?" I asked my mother this question expecting her to wipe my tears and hand me the answer, but I had come to a point in my life where I had to make the major decision.

My mother stood by me and comforted me with warm hugs and verses from the *Qur'an* until my weeping became sniffling. But my mother did not carve the answer in stone and give the stone to me. Instead, she explained to me the reasons to wear *hijab* that my little 10-year-old mind could grasp. She explained all the benifits that I would get in this life and in the hereafter from wearing the *hijab*. And then she asked me what I wanted to do.

"You will be upset if I don't wear it," I said.

"No Sweetie," my mom assured me, " we won't be upset with you."

Many times I voiced my concern about displeasing my parents. The reason I cared so much what they thought was because they had given our relationship lots of love, care, guidance, and understanding. So I wanted to make my parents happy with me. But my mom didn't want me to wear the *hijab* out of fear of my parents and so that night she reassured me time and time again that they wouldn't be upset with me if I didn't wear it.

"What about Allah?" I asked. "Allah will be mad if I don't wear the *hijab*."

"*Insha' Allah,* Allah will understand if you can't wear it right now, because you are so young and we don't live in a Muslim country," my mom told me. "Now you can get ready for it and when you grow a little older you can wear the *hijab*."

"But Mama," I responded. "Allah knows everything. So, if He picked me to wear the *hijab* now, then He knows I can. So I can do it now."

I had spoken those words through heavy tears but nevertheless, I had spoken them. The fact that I had been the one to tell my mom I would wear the *hijab* and not *vice versa* made all the difference in the world. I had made the decision myself and that gave me more confidence when I walked out of the house the next day with my scarf on my head.

I think, I was only able to make that decision because of my parents' support and continuous gentle advice at various stages of my life; and the fact that I had a role model with me every day, who never forced me to do anything against my wishes, but always led me by example.

When I arrived to school, my friends, who assumed I was my older sister, asked me where I was. When I pointed to myself , they said, "Oh, you're wearing it now. Cool!" And to my surprise life went on normally.

When I got home that afternoon, I gave each one of my parents a long hug. It was a thank you for their precious admonition and advice.

Upbringing by Punishment

When a good example and a gentle word doesn't work, parents can apply some punishment. For most children, punishment is not needed, and it should never be the first means of *tarbiyah*. Parents should be patient and try various ways and means before thinking about punishment.

Although in the *Qur'an* Allah allows punishment, He always asks the believers to try the best way in dealing with anybody.

وَمَنْ أَحْسَنُ قَوْلًا مِمَّنْ دَعَا إِلَى اللَّهِ وَعَمِلَ صَالِحًا وَقَالَ إِنَّنِي مِنَ الْمُسْلِمِينَ وَلَا تَسْتَوِي الْحَسَنَةُ وَلَا السَّيِّئَةُ ادْفَعْ بِالَّتِي هِيَ أَحْسَنُ فَإِذَا الَّذِي بَيْنَكَ وَبَيْنَهُ عَدَاوَةٌ كَأَنَّهُ وَلِيٌّ حَمِيمٌ

Who is better in speech than one who calls (people) to Allah, works righteousness, and says, I am of those who bow in Islam?

Nor can goodness and evil be equal. Repel (evil) with what is better: Then will he between whom and you was hatred become as it were your friend and intimate! (41:33–34)

ادْعُ إِلَى سَبِيلِ رَبِّكَ بِالْحِكْمَةِ وَالْمَوْعِظَةِ الْحَسَنَةِ وَجَادِلْهُمْ بِالَّتِي هِيَ أَحْسَنُ إِنَّ رَبَّكَ هُوَ أَعْلَمُ بِمَنْ ضَلَّ عَنْ سَبِيلِهِ وَهُوَ أَعْلَمُ بِالْمُهْتَدِينَ

Invite (all) to the way of your Lord with wisdom and beautiful preaching; and argue with them in ways that are best and most gracious: for your Lord knows best who have strayed from His path and who received the guidance. (16:125)

He also asked the Prophet Muhammad to be patient even with the disbelievers and what they were doing:

وَاصْبِرْ عَلَى مَا يَقُولُونَ وَاهْجُرْهُمْ هَجْرًا جَمِيلا

And have patience with what they say, and leave them with dignity. (73:10)

As a matter of fact the Prophet Muhammad said:

The best of you will never use force to deal with their families. (Abu Dawud)

He himself never used force as a means of *tarbiyah*. He used it only to fight for the sake of Allah.

So punishment does not necessarily mean using force; it means using certain disciplinary measures such as depriving children of their allowances for a certain period of time, or not allowing them to visit certain close friends for a specified period of time. It is important to notice that while applying this tool of *tarbiyah* you do it with mercy and gentleness. Children should always feel that even when punished you still love them. You discipline them out of love, as illustrated by the following examples.

The first example is narrated by our 14-year-old daughter.

I remember once being punished for not using my time wisely. At that time I felt it was unfair to be banned from TV for two weeks, but now I realize how important it was that I should learn my lesson.

My sister and I had been watching TV for two straight hours and hadn't yet prayed *maghrib*. When my mother found out, she told us to pray, and said that we couldn't watch TV for two weeks. During this time period though, both my parents gave me the support I needed and treated me normally. I could feel the consequences of my mistake because my parents' attitude toward me was as it always was. I think this punishment worked because it wasn't too harsh but at the same time it was firm and appropriate for the situation. I experienced the punishment as a natural consequence of what I had done.

Here is how our 16-year-old daughter feels about punishment.

I strongly believe that punishment is a necessary tool for *tarbiyah*. I have heard opinions which say that punishment in upbringing is unacceptable and unnecessary, and that encouragement, advise, and leading by example should be used instead. I agree that these techniques are important and needed in the practice of raising children but I think that punishment does have its place.

I am 16 years of age and attend a public high school. At school I have made many close friends, all of whom are non-Muslims. I would like to relate to you a true story, using fictional names.

Lisa Smith is a good friend of mine who has been able to avoid the drugs and alcohol scene. Both Lisa and I feel that they just damage one's life and that there is absolutely nothing "cool" about doing drugs.

This year Lisa mixed with the wrong crowd and she's been drinking a lot and doing drugs on a regular basis. Often, she complains to me that she hates getting high and she always says, "I hate it so much! Ugh!! That's the last time ever—I'm not doing this anymore!" But she can't keep herself away from it: Next weekend, she's out there getting high again.

When her mom found out Lisa was doing drugs she was shocked and disappointed. But since this is Lisa's life not her mom's, all

Mrs. Smith could do was offer her sincerest advice and encourage her daughter not to use drugs. Mrs. Smith took Lisa to many doctors who informed her of the negative effects drugs will have on her body. Mrs. Smith also offered Lisa a deal: If Lisa stayed away from drugs until she graduated from high school, then her mom would give her a certain amount of money.

Lisa felt bad and became hesitant about her use of drugs. But that only lasted a few weeks until she found herself at a party and did not resist the pressure of doing drugs again.

I am positive that if my parents ever found me doing drugs, they would punish me. They would explain why and encourage and advise, but they would also punish. Because this is a very serious subject and is life threatening. Punishment should definitely be used. Lisa could live without the bonus cash that she would receive if she avoided the drugs, but if it was a privilege she already had, she may have thought twice before giving in to peer pressure.

And here is a another real life example as told by the same daughter:

Disciplining should not only be an important part of *tarbiyah*, but should also be an important part in each parent. Parents should be able to discipline their child and still be their friend and playmate. It is not fair to leave disciplining to only one parent. Then that parent becomes the bad cop. It should be done in such a way that whoever is present at the time the child misbehaves, is the one who will deal with the misbehavior.

I have seen mothers, when their children misbehave, threaten: "You just wait until Dad comes home—I'll tell him what you're doing!" The mother has just placed the father in a horrible position. All day dad is in the office doing his work and then when he comes home he has to judge the crimes of the day and decide the fines for each crime. This way, all the kids see is a strict, firm father. If mom happens to forget about the misbehavior incident by the time dad arrives, then the children get away with their bad behavior. Also, the children will see that mom does not have authority; she has to wait until dad comes home so she can tell on them so dad will discipline them.

In my family, whichever parent is present at the time of the incident is the parent who takes on the disciplinary role. Since my father works in his office outside our home and my mother works at home, my mother is usually the one present at the time of misbehavior; therefore, she is usually the one who takes care of the disciplining.

Hitting without hurting can be a form of discipline. I will tell you of an event that I remember very well. I do not remember what it is that I did, but I do remember that I knew that it was bad before I did it. I think I was nine years old. My mom found out about this and was disappointed in me. She talked with me and tried to find out why I would do this when I knew that it was bad. I think we had agreed that my father had the right to know. So, that night, when my dad came home I sat in my room waiting to see what his reaction would be. Then he called me, "Fatimah, Come!" I walked down the stairs and I was very frightened of what would happen. As I entered the family room, I saw my father's grim face. He looked so disappointed in me! I went over to him and he asked me, "Why would you do such a thing? You know better than that." His voice was so grave. Then he took my hand and slapped it. The slap did not hurt at all—it didn't even sting! It was as gentle as when one hits a cat's paw when house training it.

Though the slap had little physical impact, it produced a huge emotional one. Tears started streaming down my face. I was so disappointed in myself! How could I do this? I did know better! But most of all: How could I let him down? How could I do this to him? At that moment I saw that my father was a person, a person who has tried so hard and been so deeply disappointed. I saw that the expression on his face was a translation of the emotions in his heart. I was very upset with myself.

My mom had spanked me much harder than that little tap my father gave me that day, but because my dad had never laid a hand on me, that little tap had a great impact on me. After that, I never did something that I knew to be wrong.

Here are other examples narrated by our oldest. She is now 20 years old. She is describing how she felt and still feels about disciplining:

Discipline is a crucial part of *tarbiyah*. Sometimes it isn't just what parents do, but also what they don't do. It is very important that when children are being punished that they know that their parents are not doing it for revenge or out of hatred. Children must know that the punishment is a natural consequence of what they did. There are a few ways in which my parents achieved this. First, whenever I did anything wrong, my parents waited until they had calmed down; therefore, before they punished me, they could think clearly and not act out of anger. Second, they always told me why they were punishing me. When parents tell their children why they are being punished, very few will say, "I'm doing this because I hate you." However, because parents usually don't explain to their children the cause of their punishment, the children usually think just that. Third, when my parents told me why they were punishing me they showed me how this would help me in the real world, for outside our home people would not tolerate irresponsible behavior. At no time did I ever feel that my parents punished me because they wanted to take revenge on me. Fourth, my parents were consistent, so it was always clear to me what was wrong because I would always be punished for it. Fifth, there were different degrees of punishment, all according to how bad my fault was. This is very important because it taught me that different actions had different consequences. Sixth, my parents did not hit me unless my fault was a very serious one, and even then the hit was more of a light tap. Because my parents didn't use this type of punishment except during serious times, I knew how serious my mistake was, even though the actual punishment wasn't a grave one. Seventh, sometimes my parents even asked me what punishment I thought I deserved, if I did something wrong. This was very effective because it taught me to discipline myself. After all, this is what all parents strive to do: Teach their children to be responsible when their parents aren't around. This ties into another point, accountability to Allah. My parents made it seem that the mistakes I committed were not just between me and them, but also between Allah and me. Again, this taught me to be responsible at all times, because even though my parents can't always see me, I know that Allah can.

Thus, it is clear from what they have said that applying some punishment may be necessary. It works, but it should not be the method of first choice. Being a role model accompanied with gentle advice is sufficient with most children in most cases. However, in some cases a little punishment is required.

UPBRINGING BY STORYTELLING

Stories have a great impact on children especially if they are suitable to the age group you are speaking to. The *Qur'an* uses stories as a means of affecting *tarbiyah* in Muslims. Dr. Qutb describes three types of stories used by the *Qur'an*. The first type are historically real, having taken place at specific times and locations to specific people. For example, the stories of the prophets Ibrahim, Musa, Isa, Yusuf, and others. The second type are factual and present a certain type of human being that does not necessarily belong to a specific individual or group, but could apply to a person or a group of people of any time and place. The third type are those that describe situations that could happen at any place or time. Through these stories, the *Qur'an* teaches us lessons.

Dr. Qutb says, "It is important to notice that the stories in the *Qur'an* are clean. They always teach a lesson, tell the truth, present the human being as a whole, with all his or her weaknesses and strengths. However, it does not elaborate on the moments of weakness and always emphasizes the positive actions of humans, such as repentance and returning to Allah, asking His forgiveness, and receiving support after making a mistake." For examples of this, see the stories of the prophets Dawud and Yusuf.

One of the reasons stories are so very effective with children, especially with the age group 2 to 7 years, is their unlimited imagination. Also, children are not fully able to differentiate between reality and fantasy. As such, parents should use stories to instill good values in their children. The best sources of good, interesting moral stories are the *Qur'an*, the biography of the Prophet, Islamic history, the lives of the Prophet's companions and those who followed immediately after them.

There are two important notes and one warning for parents who wish to get the best out of storytelling as a way of *tarbiyah*.

First, spend time learning from these great sources of inspiration. Second, for each age group, use the appropriate language. Our warning concerns the source of the stories. Verify their sources to make sure they are accurate and authentic. This is particularly important in the case of stories from the life of the Prophet or his companions.

Other types of stories which are available in public bookstores may also be useful after proper screening of language, message, and moral content.

Parents may also use their own imagination to create stories that help their children solve specific problems. In this case, keep the message subtle and surround it with interesting details that hold the child's attention. Remember, children can't differentiate very well between reality and fantasy. An example of such a story is given later in this chapter.

Below, our children describe their view of storytelling and retell a few of the stories they felt had a great impact on forming their personalities.

• Some of my fondest memories of childhood are the storytelling "sessions" I had with my parents. They could happen at any time of day or night. They served to educate, as well as amuse, and they did this quite well. When it comes to my knowledge of the Prophet's life, I attribute most of it to the stories told to me as a child; likewise, for what I know of all the other prophets, peace be upon them. As for the amusement I got from the stories, this also had a great impact on me, even if in a more implicit manner. When parents try to raise strong, responsible children, the latter often have to stand up in the face of opposition at a time when they are developing and, therefore, vulnerable. During this period, the time children spend with their parents is usually their main source of support. Storytelling provides them the opportunity of bonding with their parents as well as relieving their stress. In addition, children get a chance to see their parents as a source of fun and amusement, not just as disciplinarians. In the end, of course, it is a balance of these techniques that matter. Even now, as an adult, I still enjoy listening to stories from my parents and this shows how similar children and adults sometimes are.

• Storytelling is an effective way of teaching children a lesson. Children will listen patiently and pay attention to a story and they will remember it a lot better than a lecture about behavior. Of course, a story alone will not teach them to behave. The story should act as a way of teaching them morals. Then there should be consequences to their actions if they disobey the moral taught.

Too Many Balloons

I remember when I was a little kid of eight years, my sisters and I loved balloons. We would blow up three balloons every day and keep whining and begging our mom to blow up more. After a half an hour of playing with them, they would lay about the house, making the place look messy. Now that would have been okay if they were two or three balloons, but we had about 10 of them around the house!

I guess my mother had had enough with the balloons because one day she told us this hilarious story which I will never forget. It went something like this:

Once there was a little girl who loved balloons. Everytime her family was blowing up some balloons, she would say, "Oh Mommy, blow more and more and more, please."

"No, no," her mother would respond. "That's enough for now."

Then on the little girl's birthday, when all her friends were over at her house, her mother asked her, "What is the thing you want the most today?"

"I want to have a hundred balloons," the little girl exclaimed.

"Okay," her mom said. "You're the birthday girl!" And so the little girl and her mother and all her friends blew and blew and blew. They were going to blow a hundred balloons. They blew and blew and blew and they even blew some more. They became tired but there still wasn't a hundred balloons. So they blew more and more and more. They ran out of breath but there still weren't a hundred balloons. By the time they blew up a hundred balloons they were exhausted!

Now the room was full of balloons. "Well kids," the mother said, "now you can play with the balloons!" The kids wanted to play but they were too tired from blowing the balloons. Finally, the little girl dragged herself off the couch so she and her friends could play with the balloons. When all the tired children finally got up to play, they couldn't; there wasn't any room—everywhere they went there were balloons! They couldn't see anything, they couldn't do anything, they couldn't even play because there were too many balloons!

Soon all of the little girl's friends went home because there was nothing to do. The little girl went up to her room to sleep because she was tired from blowing balloons.

(contd. on next page)

Too Many Balloons *(contd. from previous page)*

Then, many hours later, the little girl woke up because she needed to go to the washroom. It was dark because it was late at night. The little girl stepped from her bed, her eyes still half closed. Then all of a sudden, KABOOM! The girl jumped. BAM! BOOM! KABOOM!! The little girl screamed, "Help! Mommy, there are bombs in my room. They're exploding! Help! Mommy!"

The mom came in. "What is the matter?" she asked. "There are bombs Mommy," the little girl shouted in a terrified voice.

"Oh no sweetheart," the mother said. "Those aren't bombs. Those are the balloons that we blew up, remember ?"

Ever since our mother told us this story, whenever we wanted to blow up too many balloons, she would say, "No, girls we don't want to be like the girl with a hundred balloons."

Yet another story from the same daughter illustrates how parents can create stories to correct children's problems:

Playing with the Clock

I have a friend who is married and has two children. They are five and six years old. Once while I was at her house, she was telling her kids to stop playing with their father's alarm clock and changing the time on it. I noticed that the kids weren't listening to her so I asked them if they wanted to hear a story.

Since they love stories they ran over right away and sat on either side of me. With their full attention I began my story:

"Once there was a little boy named Mustafa. Mustafa was five and a half and he loved to play with the clock in his parents' room. His parents' told him to stop but it was lots of fun so when his parents' weren't in the room, Mustafa would play with the switches and watch the hand on the clock move around and around. Was Mustafa being a good boy?"

" No," the children said.

"On 'Id, Mustafa was invited to his friend's party. Mustafa was so excited about the party. He was going to see all his Muslim friends and they were going to eat cake and play really fun games! The party was to be from seven o'clock until nine o'clock on Friday. Mustafa waited for Friday to come and he waited and waited and waited. When Friday finally came, Mustafa was very excited. He took out his new pants, shirt, and tie. He dressed and he combed his hair nicely. At five o'clock, Mustafa got bored and went into his parents' room.

(contd. on next page)

Playing with the Clock *(contd. from previous page)*

He wanted to play and his parents' weren't in the room. Then Mustafa saw the clock. He ran to it and started playing with the switch. The hand on the clock turned round and round and round until the clock said three o'clock. Then Mustafa was called to dinner so he left the room and ate.

"After dinner Mustafa's parents went to their room and Mustafa played in his room. Every ten minutes Mustafa would ask, 'Is it time to go yet?' And his father would answer, 'We've still got a while.'

"Mustafa waited and waited and waited. Then, finally, it was time to go. Mustafa sang happily in the car. He couldn't wait to see all his friends and eat the wonderful cake and play the amazing games. When they got to the house, Mustafa's mother rang the doorbell. 'DING DONG.' Mr. Riyad opened the door.

"'*Assalamu Alaykum*,' Mustafa said. 'We are here for the party.'

"'The party?' Mr. Riyad said. 'The party's over. It's nine o'clock.'

"Mustafa's mother looked at her watch, 'You are right,' she said. 'My watch says nine o'clock.'

"'But my clock at home said seven,' Mustafa's dad said. 'Mustafa did you play with my clock again?'"

"'Yes,' Mustafa said.

"'We told you not to play with that,' Mustafa's mother said. 'You see, because you played with the clock, you missed the party.' Mustafa was very sad. He wanted to go to the party so much and now he had missed it. But Mustafa had learned a good lesson and he never played with the clock again."

The two children had been listening carefully to the story. They had learned the moral and would remember it better than if I had given them a talk about listening to their parents. Now it was up to their mother to follow up on the moral by making sure that whatever they did would have its consequences.

UPBRINGING BY HABITUATION

When the small things we do become habits, they become easy to practice. However, as Dr. Qutb warns, there is a negative aspect to doing things habitually—the actions can lose their meaning and purpose and become empty and mechanical. Islam discourages this negative tendency by always reminding us of the objective and purpose of any of our actions.

Islam uses habits as a way of teaching and educating Muslims. Islam removes bad habits and replaces them with good ones either gradually or all at once. When the *Qur'an* declared the custom of killing baby daughters forbidden, it had the immediate effect of removing the habit from the people. However, on the question of drinking alcohol, the *Qur'an* revealed a gradual approach. The prohibition of alcoholic drink took three or four stages to implement. The habit was finally completely removed from permissible behavior.

As for initiating good habits such as being truthful, practicing patience, and helping others, Islam motivates the individual internally to desire and love them for the benefit that the believer and the Muslim society derive. It has established a specific format and pattern for practising these good deeds. For example, prayer is a desire from the individual to be close to Allah and to ask Him for support and strength. According to Islam, prayer is performed at a specific time and in a prescribed way. Islam also prefers the prayer held in congregation to the prayer performed alone. As for zakah (alms tax, or poor due), its inner dimension is a desire to free oneself from greed and to develop a love for helping the needy and the poor. Islam has established rules for performing these acts and it prescribes a certain percentage of money to be taken as zakah. Thus, good acts become easily practiced habits, done with clear motives.

Here are some examples of how habits can have a profound impact upon children. Again, our children relate their own experiences.

Good Habits

• One habit that I learned from my parents was never to use bad language. Many people I know use foul language even when they aren't mad, it's just their casual language. Even when my parents are upset about something they don't use bad language, they make *dhikr,* remembering Allah instead. That has helped me keep my vocabulary clean.

Another habit that I've picked up from my parents is always making *du'a.* Because my parents implemented this in me from a very young age, it is now something I do without thinking. When I was little, before eating, going somewhere by car, or sleeping, my parents would remind me: "Did you say your *du'a*?" Over the dinner table we often made *du'a'* together.

(contd. on next page)

Good Habits *(contd. from previous page)*

• Since I am left handed, my parents had to train me to eat with my right hand. There was a little trick my father used, which was "our little secret." It was to look at me until he got my attention, then tap his utensils on his plate. This was to remind me to eat with my right hand without embarrassing me since all my other sisters were right handed. Now that I'm used to it, it's a normal habit. But when I was little it was very difficult.

UPBRINGING BY DIRECTING ENERGY

Every human being has potentials and types of energy as part of his or her personality. These potentials are usually neutral. They can be directed in the right direction or in the wrong direction. For example, love and hate are forms of energy stored within an individual. They have the potential to be directed either in a positive or negative way. If this energy is not utilized in some form or another, it represents a burden on the human being and could be a source of problems to the individual. Stored energy is not healthy. Energy should be used and not stored. Islam makes sure energy is used properly. For example, Islam directs love energy toward Allah, the messengers of Allah, righteous people, parents, spouses, children and all family members. Hate energy is also directed and used rather than being stored which may cause unhealthy conditions. Islam directs hate energy toward Shaytan (Satan), evil, and bad actions and deeds.

Here is an example narrated by our youngest child, at 12 years of age:

Going to Camp

My parents have always encouraged me to direct my energy toward useful things. I'm 12 and this summer I went to a Muslim day camp. It was a month-long camp and I remember, at the beginning, I didn't really want to go. My mom gave me the choice unlike most other moms. She encouraged me to try it. She didn't just sign me up and tell me I was going. She gave me a choice and often times when you choose how you're going to spend your summer you enjoy it more. Anyway, I went to the camp and it may have taken some time but I started really enjoying it. I was having so much fun even though I was in an Islamic

(contd. on next page)

> **Going to Camp** *(contd. from previous page)*
>
> *surrounding, memorizing Qur'an, listening to stories of the Prophets, and singing Islamic songs. If my parents hadn't been there to encourage me to go or to pay for me I wouldn't have had great memories to tell about how I ended up memorizing that surah or all the fun I had with my Muslim friends. I'm not saying that if I hadn't gone to the camp I would have been at the mall everyday. No, I probably would have done Islamic stuff, but this way I did Islamic stuff that I'll always remember. Now I say to myself how could I ever have doubted going to KAMP KALEIDOSCOPE!*

UPBRINGING BY UTILIZING TIME

Spare time can be a source of problems. Ibn Abbas reported that the Messenger of Allah said, "Two blessings that the people may lose are health and spare time" (Bukhari).

Individuals who have lots of spare time, tend to use it wasting their energy and resources. To ensure that a human being reaches his or her God-given potential, time should be utilized properly and excess spare time avoided. The importance of proper time utilization is emphasized over and over in the sayings of the Prophet. It was reported that he said:

> Everyone will be asked about four things on the Day of Judgment: his life, how he spent it; his youth, how he used his time; his wealth, how it was earned and on what it was spent; and his knowledge, how he used it. (Tirmidhi)

Regulation and positive utilization of a Muslim's time is one of the main objectives of the rituals of Islam. Prayers and supplications are performed at a specific time during the day. *Zakah* payment is an annual event. Fasting is kept daily in a specific month of the year from dawn to sunset. Islam makes sure that a Muslim's day is filled with useful activities leaving no excess time for him or her. Not only is this done through prayers and *zakah*, but also Muslims are encouraged to participate in every useful action that benefits society in general. Allah says in the *Qur'an*:

وَتَعَاوَنُوا عَلَى الْبِرِّ وَالتَّقْوَى وَلَا تَعَاوَنُوا عَلَى الْاِثْمِ

And cooperate on righteous deeds and *taqwa* and don't cooperate
on bad things. (5:2)

Muslims are asked to help each other, to start useful projects to
strengthen the community, to visit the sick in hospitals, to help the
elderly, to attend funerals and visit cemeteries, and to participate
in charitable events for the poor and needy.

All these noble activities occupy a Muslim's life leaving no
excess spare time for him or her to waste. The life of a Muslim
should be one of good action and good experience, continually.
Successful parents will fill their children's time with useful and
fun activities which suit their age group.

Here are some good activities which can teach children how to
share and properly utilize their time:

- Preparation of a back-to-school box for needy children within the
  community.
- Preparation of bed-time snack box for poor and needy children
  within the community and neighborhood.
- Sweet box for *'Id*s for unfortunate children.
- Share in child sponsorship program with charitable organizations to
  help children in other countries.
- Write letters to and visit the elderly and sick members of the
  community
- Participate in boys and girls clubs regularly.
- Organize sports or other recreational events for children of various
  communities in cities within driving distance of each other.

Here is a story of how effective time utilization helped one child
to form a good, effective, and efficient personality as told by the
child herself:

Using Time Wisely

One thing that I remember is that my parents have always encouraged me to direct my energy and spend my time on useful, often Islamic, things.

When I was young, during the summers, I went to a week-long Islamic camp just outside Ottawa, Canada, called Long Bay Camp. At camp we did many recreational activities along with learning Qur'an, Hadith, and other Islamic lessons. Another thing is that at camp the surroundings were Islamic. If I hadn't gone to camp for that week in the summer, I wouldn't have learned as much or spent my time as wisely.

More recently, I have joined a swimming group called Sisters' Splash, which is a group of Muslim sisters who go swimming for two hours every Saturday. My parents encouraged me to go and paid the registration fees. This way, I got to spend time with Muslim sisters instead of going out somewhere with a non-Muslim friend.

I've also joined an Islamic singing group that performs at Islamic functions. For the last two years I have been in my school choir and have always been interested in singing. Since I have joined the Islamic singing group though, I've noticed that it's more fun to be singing with Muslim friends. The Muslim singing group has also helped me think more Islamically in general. By saying this I mean that now, when I have a tune stuck in my head, more often than not, it's the new Islamic song that I learned in the Muslim singing group instead of some love song. Again, my parents paid the registration fees and got me involved. Without my parents' encouragement, and their involving me in Islamic activities, I probably wouldn't have joined. Now, when I look back on times I've spent with my friends, I have memories with Muslim friends I can laugh about or remember. And memories are a very important part of people because they are the things that stand out in one's mind and mean something special.

UPBRINGING BY EVENTS

Utilizing events as a means of *tarbiyah* is a very powerful tool that parents can use to help their children understand concepts and acquire strong personalities. Special events, which motivate individuals, catch them when they are most receptive to advice. Allah, through the *Qur'an*, used this tool on many occasions to modify and correct the behavior of the Companions. Some of the great examples of utilizing this tool can be found in *Surat Āl Imran* (3), *al Anfal* (8), and *al Tawbah* (9) in which the battles of Uhud, Badr, and Hunayn are discussed, respectively. Here we see that the *Qur'an*, using the events of the battles, clarifies basic Islamic concepts to the believers. Among these concepts are the following:

- Victory is only from Allah. Muslims have to exert their efforts to achieve it, but be sure that the results are in Allah's hands only.
- The Prophet Muhammad is a human being and is subject to all that happens to human beings (e.g., injury, sickness, and death). As such, no Muslim should give up his struggle because of the death of the Prophet. Muslims worship Allah the Almighty, not the Messenger of Allah.
- Allah is just and fair. He does not favor any group over another. Every action has consequences and whoever commits a mistake, suffers the consequences of that mistake.
- The life for Muslims is made up of one trial after another and one test after another. Muslims should prepare themselves and understand life as such.
- The number of troops in an army is not necessarily the ultimate determinant in winning a battle.

Parents should make use of events that take place in the life of their children to link them to Allah and instill in them correct Islamic concepts. These events can cover a wide spectrum of concepts. They can be as simple as helping their child find something that he or she has lost. They also could be as complex and painful as losing one's family member in an accident or through natural causes. In both cases, it is the parents' responsibility to utilize the occasion fully, ensuring that lessons are learned by the children.

Here is an example illustrating how using events can be very helpful in forming a strong and dedicated personality. It is related by our 12-year-old.

An Event to Learn from

One event that I learned a lot from was when one of my close cousins, Wala', died. He was a cousin that I always played with. When he was around 11 years old, he got a brain tumor. I remember going to the hospital, in Egypt, just before we left for Canada. His head was shaved and he was barely conscious of what was around him. Then a couple of days after we arrived in Canada, we got a call from my uncle and his wife (Wala's parents), telling us that Wala' had passed away. My four sisters and I, especially Hoda, who was really close to him, instantly began to cry. We were all very sad and needed lots of comfort, and comfort is exactly what our parents gave us. Our parents explained to us that this life is a test and that it's okay to cry when somebody dies, after all we are human. You can cry for a while but life must go on. Don't sit and just sulk and grieve because everybody dies whether they're 80 or 18. Practise your Islam, read the Qur'an, because that's going to get you good marks on your test. And insha'a Allah, if the person who died was a good Muslim, you will see him or her again in heaven.

Summary

In this chapter, we discussed eight different methods of *Tarbiyah*. These are; modeling, exhortation (gentle advice), punishment, stories, directing and exerting energy, time utilization, inculcating habits, and utilizing events. References to *Qur'an* and the teachings of prophet Muhammad may Allah's peace and blessings be upon him and discussions of Dr. Muhammad Qutb were used extensively to support these methods. Numerous practical examples were presented to augment the theory of each method and provide the parents with leads as how to use them with our children. Several stories were also used to illustrate the importance of using stories as an important method of *Tarbiyah* for our children.

CHAPTER 5

CASE STUDIES

INTRODUCTION

In this chapter we present practical case studies, some of which we used in our parenting workshops. They proved to be illustrative and brought the point home to parents. To make the most out of these studies, please follow the instructions below exactly:

1. Read each case study carefully.
2. Answer all the questions in writing and in detail.
3. Write down any other ideas that you may have that may have not been covered in the questions.
4. After you finish all case studies go to the next chapter and compare your answers with those in the book. Don't go to the next chapter except after you finish all the cases.
5. It is beneficial to do this exercise together with your spouse.
6. While you are answering the questions try to remember the basic principles of *tarbiyah* as well as the ways and means of *tarbiyah* explained in the previous chapters.

Get ready. Have a notebook and a pen and enjoy these exercises.

A. THE FIRST DAY OF SCHOOL! (KINDERGARTEN)

Raniyah is a nice little five-year-old girl. She lives with her parents, her younger sister Hanan, and her younger brother Ahmad in an apartment building. Raniyah spends most of her time at home and sometimes she goes out with her family to visit friends from the same ethnic background, where she plays with other children her own age.

In September, Raniyah will start attending kindergarten for the first time. She is very excited about this. She can't wait to go to school because she enjoys playing with children of her own age very much. During this time, Raniyah's parents buy her new things to prepare her for school.

On the first day of school, Raniyah tries to participate in class activities and to play with the kids in her class, but she barely understands their language and she can't speak it. Because of this, she feels uneasy about playing with the other kids, and she feels that they are mean to her. Whenever she tries to play with the other children they say, "Go away. We don't want to play with you!" Now Raniyah doesn't like school and she feels very lonely there. She doesn't know how to spend her time when she's in school. Sometimes she cries and often she sits alone, far away from the other kids. At this time, Raniyah's teacher asks to meet Raniyah's parents.

Questions:

1. How do you think Raniyah feels while she is at school?
2. How do you think her parents feel about this problem?
3. In your opinion, what caused this problem?
4. What suggestions and/or solutions would you give to Raniyah's parents to help them solve this problem?
5. What suggestions and/or solutions would you give in order to prevent situations such as this one?

B. Peer Pressure and Home Expectation

Fatih is a seventh grade student. He tries his best to live up to his parents' expectations. This takes a great deal of his effort and often goes unnoticed. At school, Fatih is experiencing a lot of peer pressure and doesn't feel that he belongs. He doesn't enjoy sports, or belong to a group, or have many friends. In school one day, Fatih's only friend asked him to go with him during recess to buy something from the store. Fatih went along with his friend who bought a pack of cigarettes and started smoking. He offered Fatih a cigarette and kept pressuring him to try it. Fatih had a hard time refusing, but he managed to say no. Fatih finds it hard to cope and needs to talk about it, but he is scared of mentioning what happened, fearing that his parents will be upset with him and that his dad would be really mad. That same day, Fatih went home with his report card. When his dad looked at it, he was upset. Without asking for reasons, he scolded Fatih about two grades that did not meet his expectations. Fatih is very upset and finds it hard to meet his parents' expectations at home, and deal with the peer pressure at school.

Questions:

1. Do you feel that Fatih is in a difficult position? How would you feel if you were in his place?

2. As a seventh grade student, do you think it is important to feel like you belong to a group?

3. What do you suggest Fatih's parents do to help him have high self-respect, so he is in a stronger position dealing with peer pressure?

4. Do you think Fatih's dad is putting enough effort into having an open communication channel between him and Fatih?

5. What would be your advice to Fatih's dad to improve the situation?

C. THE MISTAKEN/NEGATIVE SUPPORT

Fayiz is nine years old. He is a fourth grade student who lives with his parents, his seven-year-old brother, and five-year-old sister. Fayiz isn't doing well in school. He has problems finishing his school work. Frequently, he runs into problems with his peers. At home, Fayiz feels bored and doesn't want to help with anything around the house. He watches a lot of TV and often fights with his brother and sister.

Fayiz is always asking his parents to buy him new things (toys, a watch, clothes) and once he gets one thing, he starts asking for another. He is never satisfied. During parent-teacher interviews, Fayiz's teacher discusses his case with his parents and says that

Fayiz has a problem accepting responsibilities, doesn't care about the consequences of his actions, and has no enthusiasm for learning. She advises his parents to follow up with him regarding his school work.

Fayiz's mother sits down with him and together they make a schedule for his schoolwork and house chores. She explains to him that if he keeps up with his responsibilities she is going to reward him, and if he doesn't he will suffer the consequences.

One day, while Fayiz is watching TV, his mother reminds him a few times that his room should have been cleaned a few days ago. She asks him to clean it before dinner. After dinner, his mother checks his room and sees that it is still a big mess. She calls Fayiz and tells him that since he hasn't cleaned his room, he will not get to eat dessert. Fayiz is mad and shouts, "That's not fair! I love chocolate cake!" At this point, his father interferes saying to his mother, "Don't be so harsh on him. He's already suffering enough. Here's your piece of cake, Fayiz. Next time be a good boy." His mother looks at them silently, not knowing what to do.

Questions:

1. Do you think Fayiz is being realistic when he expects to gain things without working for them?

2. By reacting the way he did, is Fayiz's father

   a) guiding him;

   b) pitying him;

   c) confusing him;

   d) harming him; or is he

   e) helping him?

3. Fayiz's actions show that he is:

   a) a discouraged boy who doesn't believe in himself;

   b) a well-balanced boy who can cope with peer pressure;

   c) a boy who likes to give and take;

   d) a boy who only likes to take.

4. Do you think that the way the father is showing his love and care for Fayiz is helping him? Why?

5. What advice would you give to the father?

6. What advice would you give to the mother?

D. School Activities

Jamilah is 14 years old. She is in high school. One day, *Jamilah* is in drama class. They are doing warm-up games. When it is Jamilah's turn to participate, the teacher chooses a boy as her partner. Jamila knows there may be physical contact, but is afraid to say anything. She does not want to be embarrassed in front of her classmates. Jamilah participates in the game and has to link arms with her partner. She feels bad about the incident, and discusses it with her mother. Her father overhears the conversation.

Questions:

1. What do you think was the parents' reaction to this situation?
2. How do you think Jamilah felt about herself after the incident?
3. What do you think would be the best way to handle the situation, as a parent?
4. Could the girl have done anything to prevent the situation from happening?

E. Christmas Season Art Work

Mustafa is in the second grade. His class is preparing for the Christmas season. The activities they are doing include: singing Christmas carols, decorating trees, writing letters to Santa, and making arts and crafts. Mustafa has made something beautiful of which he is very proud. When he brings it home to show to his mother. He asks her to display it on the fridge. Mustafa's mother becomes angry and does not want to put it on the fridge. Instead, she throws it in the garbage.

Questions:

1. How do you think Mustafa's mom handled the situation?
2. How do you think Mustafa felt after the incident?
3. Do you think this could affect Mustafa's self-esteem? Will this incident draw him closer to his mother who represents Islam, or closer to his teacher?
4. How do you think the situation should have been handled?
5. Could Mustafa's mom have done things to help build his self-esteem using what he made, while at the same time, encouraging Islam?

F. THE SLEEPOVER DILEMMA

Sofiyah is 11 years old. She comes home from school and asks her mother if she can sleep over at a classmate's house. Her father overhears the conversation and joins the mother in stating a very strong "No!" When Sofiyah protests, the father adds, "No girl of ours is sleeping outside of the house."

Questions:

1. How do you think the parents handled the situation?
2. How do you think the child felt after the incident?
3. How do you think the child felt toward the adults after the incident?
4. How do you think the situation should have been dealt with?

G. TO PAY OR NOT TO PAY

Fatima is a seventh grade student, she uses the bus to go to school. One day she came home crying and saying that she lost her bus pass. Her mother was very upset since it was only the fifth day of the month. She started shouting at Fatimah, using harsh words. This continued for a while until her mother said, " Go away! I don't want to see you. Wait till your dad comes home to punish you." Fatima went to her room crying. She couldn't do any of her home work. She couldn't concentrate; all she could think about was the punishment waiting for her when her dad came home.

When her dad arrived home the first thing her mother did was to tell him about Fatimah's carelessness in a very upset tone. Her dad was equally angry. The father reprimanded Fatimah rather severely for what was only an accident. To make things worse, he too shouted at her. "Where is she?" he shouted. And when she stood in front of him, he shouted angrily, "How many times did we tell you to be careful with your possessions. You are always like this. Well then, no supper for you tonight, and tomorrow you are not going to school. I'll also ask the principal to announce in the school why you are not there so everybody will know how bad you are."

The next day, Fatima's father bought her another bus pass and warned her, "If you lose this one again, you will see what will happen to you!"

Questions:

1. How do you think the parents handled the situation?
2. How do you think the child felt after the incident?
3. How do you think the child felt toward the adults after the incident?
4. How do you think the situation should have been dealt with?
5. Do you think the parents used any of the basic principles of *tarbiyah* with Fatimah.

H. LITTLE ALI AND THE JUICE

Ali is three years old. Ali often goes to the refrigerator, opens it, and stares inside. One day, Ali took the orange juice jug out of the fridge, put it on the kitchen table and poured himself a glass. While doing this, a lot of juice spilled on the table and kitchen floor. Ali's mom came into the kitchen and saw the mess. She got mad, yelling at Ali, "Look what you have done, little naughty boy." She grabbed the jug from Ali and put it on the counter. Then she took Ali to the living room where she spanked him so hard that he cried and screamed loudly. Ali's mom then went to clean the mess in the kitchen.

Questions:

1. Can a three-year-old child pour himself a glass of juice without making a mess?
2. What do you think of the reaction of Ali's mother?
3. How do you think Ali feels right now?
4. In your opinion, how should Ali's mother have reacted?
5. What do you think Ali's parents should have done ahead of time to prevent situations like this?

I. THE TOY PROBLEM
("YOU ARE THE OLDEST, YOU SHOULD KNOW BETTER.")

'A'ishah is the mother of two children—Maryam (seven years old) and Murtada (five years old). 'A'ishah takes good care of her children and would like them to grow up as friends, who love and care about each other.

Everytime Maryam and Murtada get into a fight over a toy, or a book that each one wants, 'A'ishah rushes to solve the problem for them. Usually, Murtada is crying over the toy, so 'A'ishah tells Maryam to give the toy to Murtada. She tells Maryam that since she is older, she should be more giving to her younger brother. Maryam starts crying and says, "I always have to give him my toys. I never get to play with anything!"

'A'ishah tells Murtada, "You should also stop crying about everything and share the toys with your sister because it's not fair to Maryam. I know how she feels because when I was little I always had to give my toys to my younger sisters and brothers."

Questions:

1. In your opinion, is this a common problem?
2. What do you think is causing the problem?
3. How would you advise the mother to:
   a) Solve the problem of fighting between her children?
   b) Strengthen the bond between her children?
4. Find a similar example in your life between you and your children.

J. BEDTIME

Ahmed is a only four years old. Ahmad and his parents have an agreement that his bedtime is at 8 p.m. At 8 o'clock, Ahmad's mother tells him, "Go to sleep honey. It's eight o'clock."

Ahmad pleads, "Please, can I stay up just a little longer Mommy?"

"No, you should go to sleep now," she responds as she answers the ringing telephone. After the phone call, Ahmad's mother continues her work while Ahmad keeps playing. At nine o'clock Ahmad's father notices that Ahmad is still up. "Go to bed Ahmad. Remember, your bedtime is at eight o'clock."

"Daddy, just a bit longer, please?" Ahmad says as he continues playing with his toys.

"Absolutely not," the father objects, turning back to his paperwork. Ahmad plays with his toys until his parents go to sleep.

Every night, Ahmad's parents ask him to sleep at 8 o'clock but are too busy to make sure he does. Ahmad stays up until his parents' bedtime then goes to sleep.

One night at 8:30, after Ahmad had been asked to go to sleep and he was still playing with his toys, his father saw him and said to his mother, "Didn't you already tell Ahmad to go to sleep?"

"Yes, I did but he doesn't listen at all," his mother responded.

"Ahmad," yelled his father, "why haven't you been listening to your mother? Your bedtime is eight o'clock . It's already 8:30 and your mother told you to go to sleep!"

"You never listen to me!" his mother pitched in. "You don't have any respect for what your parents say! You bad boy. Go to bed right now!!"

"You heard your mother. Go to bed Ahmad!!" his father ordered. Ahmad started to cry.

Questions:

1. Is this a common problem?
2. What do you think is the reason for the problem?
3. Do you think the way the parents reacted to Ahmad's behavior conveys the right message to him?
4. What do you think Ahmad's feeling was when his parents yelled at him?
5. What would your advice be to Ahmad's parents to solve this problem?

K. PLAYING INSIDE

Hasan is a happy two-and-half-year-old boy who lives with his parents and his four-year-old brother Salih. They live in a two bedroom apartment in a large apartment building. Hasan likes to jump and run around the apartment a lot, which often gets his mom annoyed and makes her yell at him. One day while Hasan and Saleh are running after each other, playing and laughing, they break a vase on the coffee table. Their mother comes rushing in, shouting, "Look what you've just done, you naughty boys!" She slaps each one of them on the back of their hands five times and shouts: "Go to your room, I don't want to see you. Don't come out till your father comes home."

Questions:

1. Was the mother realistic in expecting that the two children could play quietly all day long without jumping and running around?

2. Was there anything that the mother could have done to prevent this accident?

3. Was the mother's reaction to the accident appropriate? Did the children learn anything from this?

4. Was the mother fair in sending the children to their room for several hours as a punishment for such a mistake?

L. DON'T BE A PERFECTIONIST

Salimah is a first grade six-year-old living with her parents and her sister Hanan. Hanan is four years old and goes to kindergarten. Salimah likes her school and enjoys her time there. One evening the mother sat with both girls, helping Salimah to do her homework while keeping Hanan busy with her coloring book. Salimah has a school assignment to write a full sheet of the letter S. As soon as Salimah finished writing one line she showed it to her mom, who looked at it carefully and pointed out the imperfections to Salimah. The mother then asked her to erase the whole line and rewrite it perfectly. Thirty minutes later, Salimah was only half way down the page. When her mother asked her to rewrite the last letter she had written, Salimah looked at her mother. With her eyes full of tears, she said, "I'm too tired, I want to go to bed. I don't want to learn anymore."

Her mother replied, "You have to finish your homework young lady."

Salimah said, " I really can't."

The mother said, "Okay, you can have a break and color with your sister. I'll get both of you milk and cookies."

A few minutes later, the two girls ran to their mother, excited to show her the picture they just colored. The mother looked at Hanan's picture and said, "You should have stayed inside the line Hanan. Now your picture does not look good. And, look over here," she said pointing at a red spot, "you were pressing too hard on the crayon. It does not make the picture nice. Here is another picture, go and try to do better coloring this time." The mother then turned to Salimah saying, "Show me your picture."

Salimah hid her picture behind her back and started crying and screaming loudly. Her mother became upset and said, "I don't understand you! Why are you crying? I am just teaching you how to do a good job. I just want the best for you!"

Questions:

1. In your opinion, is this a common problem?
2. Is the mother's behavior for the best interest of the children, if not, why?
3. Do you think a four-year-old child can control her finger muscles to draw perfect lines?
4. Do you think a first grade child can write perfect letters once they learn them?
5. How do you think the children feel?
6. What would your advice to the mother be?

M. TIRED MOTHER
(CRYING BABY & TOILET TRAINING TODDLER)

Hasnaa' is a mother of two children—Husayn who is three years old and Riwa' who is eighteen months old. Hasnaa' spends much time and energy doing her best to be sure that her children's training and development are going well. She often runs into problems and can't find anybody to seek advice from, since she lives away from her family.

Hasnaa' has been toilet training Husayn using the same method that her mother used. This method is very cumbersome and has not been working for Hussain. Since Hasnaa' has been trying unsuccessfully for over a year, she is frustrated and feels that she has failed miserably. Hasnaa' started hitting Husayn every time he fails to control himself. She feels that hitting may not be the right way of dealing with the situation but she does not know of any alternative. Having saught other solutions, she had discussed the problem with one of her friends who had suggested that she hit her son.

In addition to this, her daughter Riwa' cries regularly and always wants her mother to be around her. Her crying and noise is a big source of irritation to the whole family. The atmosphere is always tense, and the parents are always thinking of different ways to keep Riwa' quiet.

Hasnaa' always feels exhausted, which makes her nervous in dealing with her children and husband. Deep within herself, Hasnaa' feels that she has failed as a mother and a wife. She does not have enough time to clean the house or to prepare and cook a fresh meal every day. She does not get enough sleep, so Hasnaa' does not have any energy to play with her children, take them out to the park, or spend quality time with them. She is behind in her readings and can't find any quiet time to spend with her husband.

Questions:

1. In your view, is this a common problem?

2. What do you think is the reason for the problem?

3. Why does the mother feel that she failed in carrying her duties?

4. What would be your advice to the mother with respect to:

   a) The crying problem of Riwa';

   b) The continuous exhaustion; and

   c) The tension between her and her husband.

5. Try to remember a similar situation in your life or in the life of your relatives or friends.

N. Dad Is Nice, Mom Is the Police

Faten and Sameer have been married for four years. Allah has blessed them with two daughters—Rabia, who is three years old and Thoraia, who is 2 years old. Both parents are family types. They care very much for their children and try to do the right things with the girls. Faten has a problem. She feels that the girls favor their father over her. Despite the fact that Faten sacrificed her career and devotes all her time in caring for the girls and meeting their needs, the girls prefer the company of their dad and feel happier around him. When Sameer comes home from work, the girls welcome him with big hugs, kisses, and smiles. Usually after supper he spends time with them playing. While playing, Sameer often does not care about rules. He is so involved with the game that he doesn't set any limits. Faten always has to interfere to set limits. One night while Sameer is playing with the children, they spill a glass of water in the bedroom and cause a big mess. Faten sees this and is upset with the situation. Sameer tells the children, "Let us stop the game, your Mom is upset." Rabia says, "No, don't stop the game. Ask Mom to leave the room and let us continue to play." Faten is hurt.

Questions:

1. Is it good that Sameer spends time with his daughters, or is this causing problems?

2. Do you think Faten is right to be upset and hurt, or do you think she is being too sensitive?

3. Do you think there is a problem? If yes, what do you think the source of the problem is?

4. How do you think Faten should deal with the situation?

CHAPTER 6

ANATOMY OF THE CASE STUDIES

A. THE FIRST DAY OF SCHOOL! (KINDERGARTEN)

1.   Raniyah feels lonely, sad, left out, and unwanted while she is at school. For a young child of Raniyah's age, this situation is very hard to deal with.

2.   The parents must feel very bad about the problem. Their daughter is isolated and has no social skills or language skills to handle herself in school. The parents may also feel confused, frustrated, angry, and helpless.

3.   The problem is clearly lifestyle-related. The family selected a lifestyle that isolated Raniyah and put her at a disadvantage with respect to her language and social skills. Raniyah does not go out enough; she is over-protected by her mother.

4.   Raniyah's parents have a big job ahead of them. They should do the following:

   - Provide an environment in which the child can gain necessary skills. For example, take her to a park to play where she can mix with other children and learn social skills.
   - Allow her to mix with other families outside the immediate family circle.
   - Visit her school and provide support by participating with her in supervised school activities.
   - Provide her with videos that improve her language skills.
   - Take Raniyah to Islamic activities: large groups with many kids, not only the parents' friends. In these activities, Raniyah should be left in the babysitting room with other children, even if she cries the first time. Crying will not hurt her. (The same should be done with even younger children.)
   - Get more involved with Raniyah to make her believe in herself. Give her regular encouragement.
   - Stay calm, don't push her, take it gradually, step by step.

5. In order to prevent situations such as this one, a family should never isolate itself from the society in which it is living. Gradually expose a child to society in a controlled manner. Taking very young children to Islamic activities at which there is babysitting supervision is an important step in providing them the opportunity to develop social skills. Registering children in preschool or nursery school is also very helpful in teaching them how to communicate and handle themselves.

B. Peer Pressure and Home Expectation

1. Yes, Fatih is in a very difficult position. I would feel very bad and discouraged if I were in his place. Though he is trying his best with his schoolwork, trying his best to cope with peer pressure, his parents aren't appreciating what he is going through. He would be thinking, "They don't want to listen to me. What should I do? To whom should I speak? Is there anybody around with whom I can share my feelings or at least who can listen to what I have to say?"

2. Of course it is important for seventh graders to feel that they belong to a group. The feeling of belonging is a natural need and even more pressing for children. When they are young, this need is satisfied by the family. When they reach school age, they go to school where they also have a need to belong; they don't want to feel left out.

3. High self-respect (self-esteem) can only be achieved when children feel they are loved and capable. Children have to feel that they are loved by their parents. Parents shouldn't withdraw their love from their children for any reason or for any mistake that they may make. Yes, they should teach them that everything has consequences, but they should never withdraw their love from them. Being capable has to do with the various skills that children should develop with the help of their parents. Fatih's parents have to provide the opportunity for the development of his skills. It is important to encourage Fatih for his achievements and emphasize his positive behavior, such as trying his best in school, even if he doesn't meet his parents expectations. As a matter of fact, parents should have realistic expectations for their children, appreciate their effort, and support them. This goes a long way in raising children's self-esteem. With high self-esteem, children are in a much stronger position to deal with peer pressure.

4. On the contrary, Fatih's dad is shutting off the communication channel between him and Fatih. He has certain fixed expectations

of Fatih as far as school achievement is concerned, and he is very upset when these expectations are not met.

5.   To improve the situation, Fatih's dad should do the following:

- Encourage and emphasize his child's achievement rather than criticize and be upset about the report card.
- Support Fatih by being close to him and doing things with him. This way the channel of communication will be open and Fatih won't feel that it is difficult to communicate with him.
- Have realistic expectations toward his son. This will go a long way to improve the situation. Every child has identifiable potentials. The most important thing is that Fatih should try his best.
  The results should be left to Allah and as parents we should show our appreciation for the efforts exerted by our children, even if the results are not what we hoped for. If our expectations are realistic, our children will meet them. It is important for children to feel the approval of their parents for their efforts and achievements.
- Share some quality time with Fatih. This will help both the father and the son become closer and help improve the communication between them. If Fatih feels that his father is concerned with his affairs and loves him for who he is, not for the high grades he gets, Fatih will open up and share his feelings and problems with his father. This quality time can be spent camping together, attending a ball game, working on a community project together. His father could volunteer some of his time to Fatih's school programs: Even cutting the lawn or preparing a fun meal together would qualify as quality time for Fatih.

C. THE MISTAKEN/NEGATIVE SUPPORT

Clearly, this child is discouraged. He has lost his self-esteem and self-confidence. He tries to fulfill his ambitions and himself by attracting attention through negative behavior such as fighting with his siblings and his peers at school. Let us first answer the questions in this case, then make some more analysis of Fayiz' situation, his behavior, and his parents' position.

1. Of course Fayiz is not being realistic when he expects to get all that he wants without working for it.
2. By reacting the way he did, Fayiz's father is neither helping him, nor guiding him at all. He is pitying him, confusing him, and harming him.
3. Fayiz's actions show that he is a discouraged boy who doesn't believe in himself and a boy who only likes to take and not give.
4. The way the father is showing his love and care for Fayiz is not helping him. Actually, it is hurting him and reinforcing bad habits in his personality. This way Fayiz will think that there are no consequences for his actions, and that he can always get away with whatever he wants, no matter what happens.
5. Fayiz's father needs some help. Our advice to him is the following:
    *   Discuss matters with your wife before taking any action;
    *   Never dispute the mother's point of view in front of Fayiz;
    *   With responsibility, there has to be authority, so if you are not spending much time with Fayiz, and the mother is the principal in Fayez's *tarbiyah*, give her the authority to handle situations like this to gain the child's respect;
    *   It is about time you do some reading on this subject to help your child as well as your spouse.
6. The mother is trying her best, she has discussed the matter with Fayiz and prepared a schedule for him to follow.

As we said, this is a case of a discouraged child who has lost self-confidence. He spends long hours in front of the TV because he doesn't know what to do with his time. His parents haven't helped him develop social and time management skills. He feels bored all the time. He asks for new toys, thinking that the new toy will help him get over his boredom. He also exploits the difference in views between his parents to his own advantage. The parents make a big mistake when they disagree in front of him.

The parents are not taking the responsibility of the child's upbringing seriously. They have no feeling of what is right and what is wrong for their son. Moreover, when one of them (in this case the mother) tries to find the right solution and starts to implement it, the other spouse acts as an inhibitor (as we have seen when

Fayiz's father gave him the cake). It is clear that these parents are not leading the training process. They are just acting haphazardly without any plan.

They haven't provided the positive atmosphere that could help their son to come out of his discouraged situation and help him build his confidence.

The above situation could be due to any of the following reasons:

- Little or no experience on parent's part. The solution to this lies in taking the time and effort to learn how to deal with children, and asking those who have successfully brought up their children in this society.
- The parents have no skills. As such, they themselves cannot provide the right environment in which their child could participate in activities that would help him improve his social skills and raise the level of his self-confidence.
- Falling under day to day pressures, being busy with other priorities, and neglecting Fayiz's needs in terms of training and coaching have lead to Fayiz's weak personality.
- Using the traditional ways of *tarbiyah* which clearly lack firmness and the continual follow-up required for solving the problems of today.

Here it is useful to note that Fayiz did not follow the schedule which was mutually prepared with his mother. This should not have surprised the parents. Fayiz was neglected for a long time and he is not used to fulfilling his duties. As a matter of fact, by not following the schedule, Fayiz may have been testing the seriousness of his parents in this new way of dealing with him. Parents should expect to solve this sort of problem gradually, step by step. For this approach to succeed, rigorous follow-up by parents is a must. Clearly, in this case the follow-up was too relaxed.

Again, here we emphasize that Fayiz's father should have not interfered with his mother's punishment for the following reasons:

- Fayiz has to learn the consequences of his actions.
- There is no gain without pain. It is important that children feel some short term discomfort to be able to face other problems later in life. A child who gets all that he wants, and has never been refused any

request grows up to be a very weak person who can't stand up to an obstacle.

To improve Fayiz's situation, the parents should do the following:

- Agree between themselves on a common way to follow up with Fayiz and agree with Fayiz on his duties and responsibilities; explain clearly to him the consequences of not fulfilling such responsibilities. Let him live the experience and feel the consequences.
- Provide the proper atmosphere for Fayiz so that he feels that his parents really are concerned with him and his needs through the following steps:
    - Closely monitor him in school and homework.
    - Make him participate in school activities that increase his self-confidence;
    - Eliminate his spare time so that he does not sit in front of the TV. Fill his time with sports and social activities to develop his social skills. The parents should help and serve him in participating in these activities by driving him and making themselves available to give him the support he needs.
    - Establish a good, open, clear channel of communication between the parents and Fayiz, especially the father. Fayiz needs to see an example in front of him. The logical one is his father. The father should make a friend of Fayiz.

D. SCHOOL ACTIVITIES

1. The typical parents' reaction to such situations, especially those from Eastern backgrounds, is to shout and make a big scene with their daughter for doing such a thing.

2. Jamilah must have felt bad about herself after the incident. She knows that physical contact between different genders is not allowed, yet she couldn't say no. She also must have felt that she was weak and that she couldn't face peer pressure and be different.

3. As a parent, the best way to handle the situation is to discuss calmly with Jamilah what she did. Jamilah has to realize that this was a mistake on her part and that she cannot repeat such mistakes in the future. However, it may not be enough for her to

understand that this is wrong. She may need some support from her parents to get over the feeling of embarrassment for being different and to be able to say no in a nice way or suggest to the teacher some alternatives in situations like this. This support could be in the form of offering certain solutions to Jamilah and making her part of the decision. Also, with Jamilah's agreement, the parents could schedule a meeting with her teacher during which they discuss the particular issue and Muslim children's requirements in general.

4.   If Jamilah were a strong, supported, and encouraged child, she would think of some solution with the help of her family. It looks like she was not getting enough support and encouragement from her parents to be able to say no in situations like this. So she gave in and followed the crowd from the fear and embarrassment of being different.

E. CHRISTMAS SEASON ART WORK

1.   Mustafa's mother handled the situation quite badly. She over reacted and let her anger out without providing any explanation or solution to the problem.

2.   Mustafa felt very hurt and angry after the incident. His self-esteem must have been very low because of the way his mom handled the situation. Mustafa will never be eager to show his mother any of his work in the future. It is also clear that the mother broke the channel of communication between her and Mustafa.

3.   This could definitely affect Mustafa's self-esteem. There is no doubt that the result will be a child with a low self-esteem. This incident will draw him away from his mother who represents Islam and closer to his teacher.

4.   The best way to handle this situation is for the mother to clearly explain her ideas to Mustafa and the Islamic stand regarding Christmas. The mother should then ask Mustafa what he wants to do with the art work.

5.   Mustafa's mom should not have thrown the art work in the trash. Rather, she should have praised the art work and Mustafa's efforts. She should substitute Christmas crafts with Islamic crafts and encourage this for our special holidays.

Clearly, the parents did not involve themselves in their son's public school environment. Parents should attend the beginning of the year open house or "meet the teacher" night. During the interview, they should make it clear to the school officials that during the Christmas season Mustafa can do art work about something other than Christmas. Perhaps he can make an *'Id* card instead of a Christmas card, or write a letter to Grandpa instead of to Santa.

It is also important that parents find ways to introduce Islam into the public school system. This requires some dedication and effort on their part. The following are some suggestions:

- At the beginning of any Islamic occasion (e.g., Ramadan or *'Id*), write a note to the school, describing the occasion and requesting them to announce it over the PA system.
- Organize "show and tell" in your child's class about certain Islamic events.
- Provide the school with a display case about Islam.
- Volunteer your time to supervise school activities or help with children during field trips.
- Send treats and sweets to school during *'Id*.
- Invite your child's peers to your home.

It is important that, if your child expresses his or her admiration of the beautiful Christmas lights and decorations, you don't deny these feelings, rather you acknowledge them. It is a big and foolish mistake to say that the decorations and the lights are not beautiful. As a parent, don't deny your child's reality. What you should do is to wonderfully decorate your house during the celebrations of Islamic events. Ask your child to be part of the decoration process.

F. THE SLEEPOVER DILEMMA

1. The parents handled the situation very poorly. Their answer was a strong "no" to Sofiyah without any explanation. Parents have to give logical explanations to their children in a simple and convincing tone along with the feeling of love, respect, and concern.

2.   Sofiyah must have felt very sad after the incident. Certainly, she is confused and doesn't understand what is going on, or why there was a refusal for what was, in her view, such a simple request.

3.   The child must have felt that her parents acted irrationally, very strangely, and exaggeratedly. Why this emphatic "No" to such a simple request? To a child, this does not make any sense. Other children go to their classmates houses for sleepovers, so why not her? Perhaps she sees a double standard because her parents slept over the other night at their friend's place.

4.   The situation could have been dealt with in a better and subtler way if the parents had established the rules of the house clearly to Sofiyah while she was growing up. The general rule in such cases should have been: No sleepovers at friends' houses. The exception could have been if the family is well-known by the parents. An alternative solution could be that the family initiates a sleepover or similar activity with Muslim children of close friends to compensate for the child.

Still, the question of dealing with the situation on the spot has to be dealt with:

- Parents should be very calm in these situations, children should not detect any irrational behavior from them.
- Children should not feel any anger directed at them from their parents, rather they should feel their love and concern for their safety.
- Parents should discuss such problems calmly with their children, propose solutions, and make them part of the decision.

G. To Pay or Not to Pay

1.   The parents handled the situation very irrationally, they neither showed their concern about Fatimah's problems nor taught her any lesson from this incident.

2.   Fatimah must have felt very badly after the incident. She is facing a problem and needs the support of her parents, but all they did was shout at her and humiliate her. This may shut off the channel of communication between Fatimah and her parents. In the future, if faced with a similar problem, she may resort to unethical ways rather than talk to her parents.

3. After the incident Fatimah must have felt that adults behave in a very strange manner. They don't discuss matters in a logical way and they always shout and make a big scene.

4. The following are some ideas on how to deal with the situation:

    a) Fatimah's parents should make her feel that they are feeling for her and sharing her problem. This is achieved through a genuine effort to try to solve her problem. This effort could take the form of searching for the pass with the child where it is likely to have been lost or calling the lost and found at the public school and the bus company. A thorough search in Fatimah's school bag and books could also be done.

    b) After showing concern and helping Fatimah find her pass, it is important that she learn a lesson from the incident. This lesson is one of accountability and natural consequences. The child has to learn the consequences of her mistakes. The parents should not buy a new pass for Fatimah. They should discuss with her some alternatives and decide on the most suitable one for their particular situation. Here are some alternatives:

        • If the school is not very far and the weather conditions allow, Fatimah could walk to school till the end of the month.

        • If the school is not within walking distance, Fatimah should share in buying another bus pass using part of her allowance.

        • If Fatimah doesn't have enough money in her allowance, she should do some extra house chores to compensate for the cost of the pass.

5. In this example, it doesn't look like Fatima's parents used any of the basic principles of *tarbiyah*. It is very clear they were not gentle with her, they showed no mercy, they shared no feelings or concerns, and they didn't teach her any lesson from the incident. They even humiliated her with their shouting.

H. Little Ali and the Juice

1. Obviously, three-year-old children can't pour themselves a cup of juice without making a mess and that is what Ali's mother should realize.

2.   Ali's mother reacted out of anger without taking into consideration the child's ability. She shouted, yelled, and spanked Ali and
at the sametime she cleaned the mess!

3.   Because of his mother's reaction, Ali was left in confusion and
frustration and feeling angry at her. He did not learn anything
beneficial from this experience. He didn't understand her reaction
and it is very likely that he will either fight back by repeating this
incident again or get completely discouraged and never try to do
things on his own. If the mother's reactions continue in this way,
Ali may loose confidence in himself. This may lead him to do
mischief, trying to find his place in the family.

4.   If Ali's mother chose to allow him to pour himself a cup of juice,
she should expect some mess to happen. As such she should not
shout at Ali. She should stay calm and show Ali how to clean up
the mess he caused. This way Ali will learn that every action has
consequences.

5.   To prevent situations like this, Ali's parents should have made the
rules for him ahead of time. They should have made it clear to Ali
whether he is allowed to open the refrigerator or not, whether he
is allowed to pour himself a cup of juice or not.

I. THE TOY PROBLEM
("YOU ARE THE OLDEST, YOU SHOULD KNOW BETTER.")

1.   This is definitely a common problem. It happens very often in
many families.

2.   One of the major reasons for this problem is the mother's behavior. She doesn't understand the children's psychology, their
nature, how they react to challenges, and the impact of her behavior on their future. The mother is behaving out of certain inherited habits of *tarbiyah* which she herself was brought up with. She
didn't do a proper self-search to check whether what she is doing
is proper for the mental and physiological well-being of her children.

3.   Our advice to the mother is the following:
a)   To solve the fighting problem between your children:
-    Set very clear rules of ownership. If the toy belongs to one
child, he or she has the right to allow or not allow the other
child to use it.

- If the toy is common, i.e., does not belong to a specific child, make sure that equal sharing is the rule. Set a specific time; for example, 2–5 minutes for each child to use the toy.
- Don't rush to solve a problem for your children. Allow them to resolve a situation themselves.
- Deal with your children equally. Don't favor one child over another because of age. Yes, Maryam is older than Murtada, but she is still young and she also needs to play with toys and enjoy her own toy.
b) To strengthen your children's bond, in addition to the above, you can do the following:
- Observe fairness in all your actions with them.
- Provide them with games and toys that can only be played by more than one person. This will teach them cooperation and improve their social skills.
- Tell them some stories about the importance of cooperating and the importance of bonding together. See examples in "Ways and Means in *Tarbiyah*."

The mother should realize that her behavior may have a negative impact on both children. Maryam may feel that her mother loves Murtada more than her. And Murtada will grow to expect that he can always get whatever he wants. In the real world, he will be shocked.

J. BEDTIME

1. This is a common problem, especially for parents who are too busy to follow up with their children. Naturally, Ahmad would love to stay up a little longer. He doesn't want to miss anything happening in the house and would like to stay up till everybody else also goes to bed. Ahmad doesn't know that at his age his body requires more rest than adults and that is why he has to go to bed early. His parents should realize this and be firm in applying the rule.

2. The reason for this problem is two fold. First, Ahmad's parents need to apply rules to him so firmly that they become retine and he doesn't even think about breaking them. Both parents are too busy; they do not follow up with Ahmad to make sure that the rules are applied properly. Second, children like to know their limits in all situations. The moment they know how far they are

allowed to go, what is allowed, and what is not, they become very comfortable with themselves and their surroundings. Children always ask for more till it is made clear to them in a nice and firm way that there is *no more*. Ahmad's parents should have made it very clear that there is a limit and that he can't exceed it.

3.   The way Ahmad's parents reacted to his behavior certainly conveys the wrong message to him. They just vented their anger and humiliated him without any clear reason. If the parents continue to act this way, Ahmad will continue asking to stay up a little longer.

4.   Ahmad felt bad when his parents yelled at him. He doesn't understand their behavior. Almost every night they allowed him to stay up later than 8:30 p.m. He probably thought, "Why are they mad at me tonight? Those adults don't behave logically. What happened to them? What did I do to make them shout and yell at me? I have been a good boy and I was playing quietly without disturbing anybody. It is very confusing, I can't understand what is going on. Can somebody please explain to me?"

5.   What Ahmad's parents did is completely wrong for the following reasons:

   a)   You are old enough to know that, as a young boy, Ahmad needs enough time to sleep. In the way you handled Ahmad, you did not consider this.

   b)   By allowing Ahmad to pass his bedtime, you have been very loose with him. The bedtime rule doesn't mean anything anymore. This teaches Ahmad that you don't mean what you say. This is a big mistake parents often fall into.

   c)   Not being firm caused Ahmad to take things lightly. When you were harsh with him, he became confused.

Show Ahmad some firmness with gentleness. In a quiet, nice way, with a firm voice, insist that he be in bed on time. Repeat this many times, but again in a nice, gentle and at the same time, firm way. If Ahmad refuses, hold his hands gently and walk with him to his bed and put him in it. If Ahmad refuses to go with you, give him the choice by saying, "Would you like me to carry you or do you prefer to walk yourself?" Count from 1 to 10, giving him a chance to think. If he decides to walk by himself, fine, if not, carry him. Even if he cries, insist that he stay in bed.

We emphasize that you should be gentle, calm, and quiet, not nervous or harsh, shouting and showing anger at him. Here are a few tips to help you make this technique successful:

1. Firmness should be the common practice and the norm; it should be applied regularly and not occasionally to make sure that the child understands the rule.

2. The general atmosphere of the house should be quiet, conducive for the child to sleep.

3. Occasionally, the child should be allowed to stay up later, especially on occasions like *'Id* or a visit from close relatives.

4. Parents should allow 15–20 minutes a day at bedtime to spend with the child near his bed narrating a story from the *sirah* of the Prophet or reciting Qur'anic verses.

K. PLAYING INSIDE

Parents need to set clear, precise boundaries and be consistent in applying them. This will enable children to be comfortable behaving within them.

1. The mother was not being realistic when she expected Hasan and Salih to play quietly all day long without jumping and running around. Children of that age need to jump and run around; they can play quietly or read for only a limited time, after which they need to exercise their muscles through running and jumping. Forcing children to sit quietly constantly does not promote their healthy growth.

2. The mother could have done the following to prevent this accident:

   a) Take the children out regularly to either a park or for a walk to give them the opportunity to jump and run around.

   b) Take the necessary steps to ensure that the apartment or house is child proof; for example, keep all dangerous, breakable, and valuable objects out of the children's reach.

   c) Set up a place where children can jump freely and safely within the home, for example, an old mattress on the floor of one of the rooms.

3. The mother reacted toward the children out of anger and frustration. Yelling and shouting at the children is not proper behavior.

Instead, she could have explained to them why it is not safe to run around the house and get them to help her in cleaning up the mess.

4.   Sending the children to their room for several hours as a punishment for such a mistake is not fair. Parents should control their anger and not over react. Instead, they should do *dhikr* for a few minutes to cool off and decide on the proper reaction, then talk to the children accordingly.

L. DON'T BE A PERFECTIONIST

1.   This is a common problem, particularly among caring parents.

2.   The mother's behavior is not in the best interest of the children. It will discourage the children from learning and being creative. It will also lead the children to lose confidence in themselves, leaving them with low self-esteem.

3.   A four-year-old child has not yet developed a sharp, fine, muscular finger movement to be able to color carefully inside the lines.

4.   A first grader can't write perfect letters from the beginning. She will be able to reach that level over a long period of time. The last line she will write will be better than the first, but parents should not expect it to be perfect.

5.   The children feel frustrated, discouraged, and overtired.

6.   My advice to the mother is to get to know more about child development. This will help her to have realistic expectations for the children. The mother should praise the children's efforts, and avoid expecting perfection which is beyond their ability. Mother's focus should be on teaching her children good work habits, and not on getting perfect results. Encouragement is a crucial element in a child's healthy development and should not be ignored by parents.

M. TIRED MOTHER (CRYING BABY & TOILET TRAINING TODDLER)

1.   Hasnaa's problem is common among young mothers.

2.   The problem is being caused by Hasnaa's inexperience and the new situation she is facing as a young mother. She finds herself alone, facing a big responsibility of training her son and taking

care of the second baby at the same time with no previous experience. Her knowledge to deal with such a situation is very limited.

3.   Most young parents underestimate the amount of work and time required to take care of babies and young children. Because of this they don't adjust properly to the needs of their new lifestyle. As such, moms find themselves overworked and very tired, and often have no clue as to how to deal with the situation. This makes them feel that they have failed miserably in fulfilling their responsibility.

4.   Here is my advice to the mother:

a)   Increase your knowledge of child rearing, and when baby Riwa' cries, check if she is hungry or needs a change. Mom, make sure that the baby is fine as far as these two areas are concerned, after that, let the baby deal with her own situation. Do not carry Riwa' or be around her all the time. Do not shout at the baby when she cries, just ignore her. Baby Riwa' needs to learn to cooperate with the family situation, which in this case means to take care of herself, and learn not to cry and scream because mom is not paying full attention to her.

b)   Regarding Hasnaa's feeling of being exhausted, she needs to discuss the matter with her husband. The two of them should come up with solutions to adjust their lifestyle to the new situation. For example, the father could help by preparing a simple supper twice a week, or by taking one child for an outing while the mother is caring for the second child or resting and catching up on her sleep. They should make a plan and apply it with cooperation.

c)   When Hasnaa' and her husband apply their plan, she will have a much better chance of getting enough rest, which in turn will help relieve her stress. Certainly, this will have a positive impact on the tension between her and her husband.

N. DAD IS NICE, MOM IS THE POLICE

When parents do not have the same policy toward their children, this can cause problems. In this case, although Sameer spends time with his children, which is the dream of all moms, his wife Faten does not appreciate that he does not follow the rules she has set for their daughters. He lets them make a big mess when they eat without directing them to eat properly. While playing with the girls, Sameer gets so involved and everybody is really having fun, but the only problem is that he lets them go overboard. They may splash water on the mirror or on the floor; they may jump on the couches and whatever makes them happy is OK with Sameer.

When Sameer doesn't follow up on the rules with the girls, he puts his wife in a bad situation. She has only two options. The first is to take the police role and interfere to set the limit, while her husband and the children are having so much fun, which causes them to favor their dad over her. The second is to forget about training her children on good manners, so they don't think that she is mean and no fun. Faten doesn't think—and rightly so—that either choice is good or healthy for her family.

Although it is wonderful that Sameer is spending time with the girls and knows how to communicate with them, he should put some effort into following up and observing the rules.

To deal with this issue, Faten could set a meeting with Sameer to discuss the situation together. Faten should start the discussion by telling Sameer how happy she is that he has a good relationship with their daughters. Faten should then explain to him how much effort she is putting into training the girls on good manners. She should point out to him that she needs his help to follow up on the training while he is with the girls. In a nice way she could also point out to her husband, her fear that the kids might undermine her authority and not listen to her if he continues to deal with them the way he does. Both could agree about a secret word that she could use to remind him whenever the girls go overboard while playing with him.

CHAPTER 7

MEET OUR FAMILY

In this chapter we will treat you to something completely different. So far we have presented the principles of *tarbiyah*, the ways and means of *tarbiyah,* and ample case studies to apply these principles. In this chapter, the product of our *tarbiyah* process will speak to you. The results of following these wonderful guidelines given by *Qur'an* and the teachings of the Prophet will talk to you.

The rest of this chapter is completely written by our children. They will talk about themselves, their relationships with each other, and their experiences with some Islamic activities. You will also sample some of their poetry. Most of their poetry is related to the value system they were brought up to beleive in, and describes certain family relationships and real life experiences.

Now, let us meet Sumaiya, the youngest, she is 12 years old.

Al salamu 'alaykum. My name is Sumaiya. I want to tell you a little bit about my family. First of all, I have three sisters, a mom, and a dad. My sisters' names are Amirah, Hoda, and Noha. Amirah is the oldest; she's 20 years old. Though she's eight years older than me and quite busy, that has never really stopped us from playing or talking with each other. Amirah is not the type of older sister that makes you pay a dollar if you step a foot in her room without asking. No, she's actually totally the opposite. She always tells us to come sit with her, or, on weekends she'll come sleep in the room I share with Noha, so we can all talk together. She lets us borrow her stuff practically whenever we need. Even though Amirah and I don't have everything in common we are still great friends.

Then there's Hoda. Hoda and I are very similar in our personalities. Now that's the hard part. Being similar makes us the best of friends sometimes and the worst of rivals other times. But when we are the best of friends or just regular friends, which is most of the time, we have a lot of fun together. Which means I don't always have to be at a friend's house to have fun. I can be right at home, having fun while doing my homework and helping with the chores. Also my parents don't have to be worrying whether I'm safe or not. On the other hand, when Hoda and I are the worst of rivals, it's not really that bad because we always settle our differences, or should I say, similarities. Hoda and I know that our relationship is a blessing and a gift. So, no matter how bad the fight is, we always work it out and then we always realize how foolish it really was. The good thing about these fights is that they always give us a good laugh. Anyway, we have out-grown these verbal fights and we always fall into the best of friends category.

Then, finally, there's Noha. Noha and I are similar in some ways and different in others. I find Noha to be a genius. She's good in almost everything she does. But at the same time, Noha is so humble that if you didn't know her in her work, you'd think of her as a totally "normal" person, rather than as a genius, that is. She's very talkative and makes friends quite easily. I don't know, but I find that even if Noha enjoys something more with another person, she'll still make it exciting when she's doing it with you. Noha loses her temper easily so its always been a temptation for me and Hoda to bug her and see how she gets annoyed. But Noha and I, being the two youngest and with whom I share a room, know a lot about each other—we have a great relationship.

And now about my parents. I really really love and respect my parents. Now, most people would think that children love and respect their parents if they give them everything they want. No. Doing that not only makes the children greedy, selfish, and spoiled, it also makes them the boss. That is definitely not how my parents earned my respect. My parents didn't force me into too much stuff. Come to think of it, I can't remember a time when my parents didn't let me choose. For example, when I came to wear the *hijab,* my mom didn't say, "You must wear it because its your religion." She explained to me why we wear it and that sometimes it may not be the most com-fortable thing, and that wearing the *hijab* in summer doesn't mean wearing a sweater and jeans. No, you can wear light flare pants that let the wind go through them and a light button up. This way, when your friends ask you why you wear it, you can actually give them a reason that *you* believe in, not the standard line, "It's part of my religion and my parents make me wear it." I've actually had a couple of people tell me, "I should wear one of those" after I've told them why I wear it. Anyway, I've always been really comfortable with my parents. That doesn't mean I can't live without them but I really love and respect them. Even when I'm mad at them, for some reason I always end up respecting them more.

I really love my family and I'm glad that I can tell them almost everything. My sisters and I have a great bond together. But the best thing about my family is that we're all equal!

Next, let us meet Noha, she is the second youngest, she is 14 years old:

Our family consists of four daughters, a mother and a father. My oldest sister is 20 years old, her name is Amirah. Amirah is in her second year of university. Although she has become very busy over the last few years this is when I've gotten to know her best.

All my life Amirah has been the big person who is always two paces ahead. Because she is a whole six years older than I, she always seems mysterious. She is very logical and reasonable about everything. Amirah is a very organized and busy person. Most of the time I see her doing something. Amirah keeps very busy with school work, but she is also involved in the MSA (Muslim Students Association) at Ottawa University where she is a student. I can see that Amirah takes it upon herself to get things done.

Amirah and I aren't extremely close but we get along very well. Although we are two very different personalities we have found a way to deal with each other well and respect our differences.

Hoda is 16 years old and is in eleventh grade. Hoda is a perfectionist in many ways. She is very much a born leader and reminds me of my mother a lot. She and I are best friends.

Hoda is very busy with school work and other activities. She is a volunteer at an Arabic Saturday school and was a counselor at a Muslim day camp last summer. Children love Hoda and she loves them. She is a very motherly kind of person. Hoda isn't loud like me, but she isn't shy either. She has a way of speaking that gets your attention and makes you listen without having to yell or shout.

Hoda is very talented in many ways. She is an excellent student and a very good poet. She keeps an average of above 90%. Several of Hoda's pieces have been published in newsletters and other places. Hoda is very involved with the Muslim community. Her specialty is children.

Sumaiya is twelve years old and in the seventh grade. Sumaiya is sort of the family clown, but although she is, she can be very shy with people she doesn't know well.

Sumaiya is extremely Islamicly conscious. She is always there to remind me when I'm doing something wrong. Though she is the youngest, she doesn't let herself be over shadowed, and expresses herself well. Sumaiya and I have always been the "two little ones," so we know each other quite well.

Sumaiya is very talented. She is a wonderful actress, has a great voice and she's a pretty good writer too. I've noticed that people really enjoy being around Sumaiya because of her fun attitude and agree-ability. Sumaiya earns peoples' respect because she shows them that she is not afraid of what they think. She is not a crowd follower, but really thinks for herself.

After reading these descriptions you might be thinking that I have made my sisters out to be perfect, which of course they aren't, and, anyway, no one can be. I am not saying that they are perfect in any way. In fact, we are all very ordinary. I don't get along perfectly with any of my three sisters and that's just fine. It' s natural.

Amirah and I get along pretty well except at times when we are frus-trated with each other. Hoda and I are also usually just fine, but at times I feel like I can't stand her. Because we know each other so well, it's just natural that we'd know more of each other's faults. Sumaiya and I are also usually great friends except when we just can't agree or get along. It's okay that we don't get along perfectly as long as we still treat each other properly even when we are upset with each other. We are careful not to let our conflicts get between us too much and we try to keep in mind that it's usually only a small argument.

Whenever I tell a friend about something I did, and I mention my sisters, they seem surprised. They say, "You go places with your sisters?" or "You get along with your sisters? I can't stand my sisters." And when I tell them that my sisters are my best friends, they are even more surprised. It just shows me how lucky we are to have been raised up to love each other and get along. I am very fortunate that my parents made sure that we could get along and find ways around our differences. It is very important to be able to turn to your family in times of need. For that there has to be a good family struc-ture. I am glad that I am so comfortable with my family. *Al hamdu li llah.*

Here is a sample of Noha's poetry:

Daddy

A father is a friend, and a helping hand
A teacher who explains, so I'll understand;
He's nice and fun and not hard to approach
He's my tennis trainer and my soccer coach.
He's a smile forever and the special touch
That gives me confidence in so much;
He helps me stand tall and keeps me strong
He shows me the difference between right and wrong.
He is the captain of my boat
Steering correctly so we'll stay afloat;
He's the role model I've strove to follow through life
Keeping happy and positive, even through strife.
He's the guard that keeps the bad things away
He's the rainbow that follows a wet, stormy day;
He's everything funny, he's riddles and jokes
And just out of the fridge, diet caffeine-free cokes.
He's the greatest inspiration, I've ever had
But most importantly, he's the best-ever dad.

Now, let us meet Hoda, the second oldest daughter. She was 16 years old when she wrote this.

Al salamu 'alaykum! In my eighth grade "family studies" course, a family was defined as "a group of people living in the same house." The dictionary defines family as "those that live in the same house, including servants; father and mother and children; those with other relations; children as distinct from their parents; those descended from a common ancestor; a race, a group of peoples from a common stock."

I'm terribly relieved that my family has more to it than those definitions. To define my family, I would say "those with relation; those who love and take care of you; those who teach you; those who support you; those who help you in the name of Allah." My family is my conscience and my shadow. They are that pot of gold which people often wish they had and say they will search for. But my pot of gold does not need to be sought—it's been with me since my birth.

Ingredients in my pot of gold include Mama, Baba, Amirah, Noha, and Sumaiya. My oldest sister, Amirah, is four years older than me. During my early childhood and up until my entering high school, she has acted as a mini-role model to me. I looked up to her, and asked her opinion of everything I did. Upon entering high school, I used to cry and complain to her. She was my support for this enormous change I was undergoing. She took the time off her OAC (Ontario Academic Credits) year in high school to listen to my concerns and complaints, and ease the shock I was going through. I'm sure that when I begin university she will be the one I seek comfort from for this overwhelming change.

I have another sister who is two years younger than I, named Noha. Noha and I are both creative and dramatic. We love to write poetry, character sketches, journal entries, and short stories. The only thing I enjoy more than writing different pieces, is sharing those pieces with Noha and Mama. Noha is very talented in many areas. She has excellent marks in school, is involved in all sorts of extra-carricular activities, has tons of friends and still manages to keep her feet on the ground without any trouble at all. Instead of going around bragging about past achievements, Noha keeps her focus and strives for future goals. I think this is because Mama and Baba have taught us that the end is the Hereafter. Even if Noha graduated with honors from every program offered at Harvard University, she wouldn't sit and rest. Because she has so much knowledge and talent it would only increase her responsibility to do something useful with it. She would know that the next step would be using her knowledge to set up different programs and services in the Islamic community.

Noha and I are very close. We are basically inseparable when we can afford it. (We go to different schools.) When she arrives home from school, even if we know that we have too much homework to talk to each other, we sit in the same room and do our homework because we miss each other so much. The friendship that I have with Noha is very important to me. She understands my values and so I can talk to her about anything. We have a great deal of trust in each other. When I tell her something confidential, I never worry about who else might find out. I know that my secret is quite safe with her. She also understands my individuality, which is very important to me because I don't feel that I really belong in any of the groups of friends which I have.

My youngest sister, Sumaiya is a lot like me. When we were younger, our similar personalities caused fights and constant clashes. But now, with time and guidance from our parents, we avoid these clashes by compromising and setting up rules which we both agree on. Since I'm not always busy yelling at Sumaiya anymore, I've discovered some of her great qualities. I have a high stress level and so, I need someone who doesn't take everything so seriously. No matter how many things are due for tomorrow, Sumaiya can always make me laugh. And she relaxes me by doing really silly things that neither one of us would do around anybody else. (Trust me, nobody else would appreciate them!!)

My parents have always led by example and believed in letting us experience the consequences of our actions. At the same time they taught us everything they could and listened to us when we had worries or thoughts that we wanted to share. Mama is a doctor and Baba is an engineer, and both are community leaders. You may think this is a family where the pressure for excellence is brutal and that is why my sisters and I all have A averages. But you would be wrong.

In our family, the rule is that we try our best and that is all. When I am worried about an upcoming test (which I always am), Mama tells me, "Just do your best and leave the rest up to Allah." I thought it was just her way of calming me down but I found out she was serious when I got a French test back that I had studied very hard for and did not get such a great mark on. My level of comprehension in French is low, though I try very hard. Since it was a comprehension test, I did not do very well on it. My parents accepted that. In fact, I was much more disappointed than they were, and so they suggested that maybe I should read French books to improve my comprehension.

Three years ago, I auditioned for the Literary Arts Programme at a special high school named Canterbury. I didn't make it, which was a disappointment, but hey, life goes on. Just last year, Noha tried out for the Literary Arts Programme and the Dramatic Arts Programme at Canterbury and made it into both programs then chose to pursue the Literary Arts. I should be enraged, right? How could she? She made it into both?! I can't believe it! She's not that much better than I !! I hate this! I hate this! *I hate this!*

However, that wasn't how I felt at all. I was happy for her. And when I congratulated her, it was from my heart not through gritted teeth. After a while I actually started to wonder, "Why aren't I jealous? Why aren't I mad? Am I normal?" I could have hated her good fortune. I could have seen her victory as my loss. I could have been consumed by jeolousy, and this could have been viewed as being normal. Luckily, my parents had showed me how never to compare my failure to get into Canterbury with her success. Even when my parents are upset with me, they never use my sisters' achievements against me or to influence my decisions. Mama and Baba recognize each one of us as a different person with her own strengths and weaknesses, which enables us to recognize ourselves, and which enables me to treasure my pot of gold.

Here is a sample of Hoda's experience in one of the Islamic camps when she was 16.

Parents who try to protect their children sometimes become over protective and pass up chances for their children to develop their personality, skills, and maturity. I'm not talking about parents who are trying to protect their children from danger in terms of safety, rather, parents who try to protect their children from mistakes. Often they will not allow their children to take on responsibilities because they fear that their children will mess up somehow. The parents always say, "My child can't do that; he's never done anything like that before." Well, hey, there's always a first time. It is better for children if the parents let them take the responsibility and clarify the importance of responsibility to them. The parents should let their children know that they are ready to help and guide them, if they need it.

My parents trusted me with a responsibility and encouraged me to be a councilor at an Islamic summer day camp—Kamp Kaleidoscope. I can honestly say that working at the camp taught me a lot about social skills in the workplace, broadened my awareness of needs in the Islamic community and improved my creativity and organizational skills. It was also a great chance to meet many Muslims in the community that I had not known before.

At the end of the camp, the campers presented an evening of performances to their parents. I, along with two of the assistant councilors, were chosen to organize the program for this evening. Now, it was my very first time to do such a big thing but, with help and support from my two wonderful parents, my sisters, and the Camp Kaleidoscope coordinator, the evening was a great success. I was the one presenting the opening statement and so I took that opportunity to tell the audience how I felt about the Camp. I stood up on the stage in front of the many eyes and read into the microphone my many times practiced poem:

> *Al salamu 'alaykum*
> Peace be upon you all.
> As Muslims there's a responsibility
> which on our shoulders does fall.
> That is to let others know
> of the blessing with which we've been blessed,
> That life is not just a parade to show off in

a series of fest after fest,
That we must not walk barefoot
but be prepared to do our best,
Because life is not a playground to play in
but it is a very big test.
But before we can spread this message to others,
we must know it ourselves and teach one another;
We must equip our children
with values and skills
Which they can use
to climb the many hills;
Hills like pepperoni pizzas, Christmas, Halloween,
Like school dances and other events for the "maturing" teen.
When you say "no" to Christmas parties,
you can say "yes" to an *'Id* one;
Show them that wearing a scarf and praying
can come hand in hand with fun;
Teach them that they can be proud to be a Muslim
and play with non-Muslims as well;
Teach them that they can stand right-side-up again
even after they fell.
With Allah's guidance,
they can stand strong and free;
And if they ever feel like
"Ahh! The whole world is looking at me!"
Tell them, "So what?"
Let them look, let them see
What a wonderful person
Islam will make one be.
But don't forget to instill this
in your children when they're young;
Let them feel that Islam to one
is like air to one's lung.
Many parents may ask
"But how would I do that?"
Instead of watching TV or practicing piano
to perfect their E flat
Encourage your kids to watch Adam's World

or read a Young Muslims magazine
There are Islamic Activities to keep them busy
from infant hood to their teen.
Put your babies to sleep
to the sound of Qur'an
So it'll be instilled in their souls
and protect from Shaytan
Take your toddlers to picnics
benefiting Islamic foundations
Where they'll play and meet Muslims
from many different nations.
When they're five and above
they can join Camp Kaleidoscope
And, Insha'a Allah
we'll be a step in building hope,
For future generations
in the Islamic Community
Because they can reach far
the roots of one tree.
We're proud to offer an environment
where your child is secure,
And the morals and the language used
are clean and also pure.
The Islamic values
are present clear and bright
As the kids learn *du'a* before eating
or before they sleep at night.
We talked about sharing, respecting our parents
and we talked about the *rasul*
But though we learn things here at Kamp
This is not a school.
There was time to play, time to swim,
and there was time to just relax;
We made pizzas, milkshakes, and cupcakes
then ate all our delicious snacks.
We made teddy bears, played gym
and we made wooden bowls,
The beautiful atmosphere here

really touched my soul.
When I looked around me
and saw children of all ages
Of many different languages
and multiple races,
They all shone
with one distinct beauty
Which showed me a vast
and limitless sea;
Containing waves of potential
in its waters
They were all Muslim
and that is what matters.
There was no swearing, gossiping
or any of that bluff
Not like at school,
where using only clean language is tough.
I watched the children make new friends
and learn new skits and songs
They swam, made sand castles and cooked
they learned and played all day long
Before eating we'd say Bismillah
and everyone ate with their right hand
After doing *wudu*, we would make *Ikama*
then for prayer quietly stand.
Each child had a different personality
a different way of seeing things
Some liked dressing up, some liked to cook
others liked to sing;
All of them liked Qur'an time
and saying *du'a* before we ate
As I watched the kids, individuals then in groups
I saw a Kaleidoscope so great.
A Kaleidoscope is a toy in which each bead,
each child, is different from the other
But the beads as a group, the children,
form beautiful shapes when they join one another.
This toy, the Kaleidoscope,

it does not work without light
And we Muslims, without Allah's light,
cannot walk the darkness of the night.
A Kaleidoscope's a toy
and toys are fun
And we wanted joy in the Kamp
for all the little ones.
Al hamdu li-llah, I learned from this Kamp
and worked like never before
But it has all paid off and you'll know what I mean
when you see what we've got in store.

Here is another sample of her poetry when she was in sixth grade:

My father has always been very busy so he couldn't spend endless hours with us. But he did make sure to talk to us and take us out on shopping trips and he always ate dinner with us unless he was out of town. One time, when I was in sixth grade, Dad took me out to see his office at work and then for a shopping trip. I wrote this for him.

Oh Daddy

Oh Daddy, I think you're the best
I'll do you any favour—just request.
I hope we'll stay close
make a bond for the most
Stick together with tears
Stick together in fears.
Together we can go through hardships
And best of all our friendship
Which I hope will never have an "endship".
Going shopping together and to the BNR
I think we're pretty close and won't get too far,
Driving down Island Park
We've got no hatred, not a spark.
We can talk about society, girls and boys
yet all the time we're both the same voice.
We can also have fun
making hot cross buns,
On and off go the lights

But we get no fright.
When together we're happy
at bad times we make it snappy.
Everyone has problems, let's make them the least
While enjoying ourselves, we can have a great feast.
We'll give to the poor and read the *Qur'an*
Our Islam growing stronger together we'd stand.
I love you lots and hope you love me as much
Whatever you say, deep down, I'm touched.
I say this with confidence—that's what it's about
'Cause I feel it all inside me, of course, with no doubt.
So stand by me on land or sea
We can eat any steaks and defeat all earthquakes.

Finally, let us meet Amirah, our first child. She was 20 years old when she wrote this.

My family is one of the few valuable things to me in this world. The best thing about it is that we are so close and, even more importantly, that we are a strong unit. I know that this is true because of what my parents put into building and nurturing our family while my sisters and I were growing up. I can truly say that my closest friends are my family.

My parents set the foundation for our family. They combined their sense of humor and their love for the lighthearted and fun things in life with their determination to teach us the ethics and morals of Islam. But it was more than that. They taught us from the *Qur'an* and *sunnah* of the Prophet, by example. At the same time, they taught us how to think, an invaluable tool in a world that is changing significantly by the second. Words cannot express the value of what my parents gave me, my sisters and my family as a whole. I know that everything happens under the will of Allah, but, nevertheless, Allah doesn't help he who doesn't ask for it. This is why I love and like my parents so much, because they made sure that when my sisters and I grew up, we would be ready to help the world, that we would never lose our religion, and that, regardless of how physically far we were from each other, we would always be close at heart.

Hoda, is the second oldest in our family, and she is four years younger than I. She was my first best friend, and rightfully so. It may be surprising to know that she and I are as different as night and day. Nevertheless, this, I found, only strengthened our friendship. The thing that strikes me the most about her is how talented she is with children and how she adores working with them. I have no doubt that she will be a wonderful mother. She is also an extremely talented writer and poet. She has always been determined to put her best into whatever she chooses to do; she literally works it to death. This is what has convinced me that whatever she puts her mind to, she will excel at it.

Noha, in many ways, is similar to Hoda. There are six years between myself and her. She is a wonderfully sociable and creative person in drama and writing. This is why she and Hoda are so in tune. Together they can and do make everything from exciting to deep and thought-provoking pieces. The best thing about Noha is that she can always make me laugh. She is brave, in that she will get to know anyone and everyone, in a matter of minutes and for that reason, many people will warm up to her in no time. Because there was such a big age difference between myself and Noha, it was only recently that we got to know each other as individuals.

Sumaiya, eight years younger than me, is my "little mommy." The reason I say this is because, when we were children we would pretend that I was her daughter and that she was my mother. Sumaiya has always had the mothering instinct. She, too, enjoys working with children. She, too, is artistic, but more in the visual arts. And because she pays attention to detail, anything she does is done well. Even though there has been a large age difference between myself and her, we developed a relationship early. Maybe it was because when she was born, I was old enough to take care of her and so a bond was developed immediately.

Like every family, we are a group of individuals who have many similarities and many differences. We all have our weak and strong points. The ability to complement each other, instead of letting our differences divide us, is what I like most about my family. Of course, the best way to do this is by understanding Islam and most of all the

Prophet, for he and his family were the best example. On more concrete terms, there were certain things that our parents did to make sure that our relationships with each other as siblings were deep and sincere ones. For example, they never compared us to each other. They recognized that we were different individuals with our distinct strengths and weaknesses, that we did not have to all excel at the same things. At the same time, this did not mean that we weren't encouraged to reach our highest potential and to put our best effort into it. The key factor here is that they recognized that each of us had different potentials in different things, and this did not make anyone of us better or worse than anyone else. To make sure that this was the message we got, we were all treated equally. We all received the same amount of attention and the same value of attention. By value, I mean that we each received attention where we cherished it most, and because we were all different, we all cherished certain types of attention differently. *Al hamdu li-llah,* I have been blessed with this, and it is my family which was my foundation, and without which I would not be the happy *Muslimah* I am today.

SUCCESS AND FAILURE SURVEY

The following few points are the result of a survey that we conducted with our children. The purpose of the survey was to find out where we succeeded with the children and where we failed. We asked the children to list all the points they liked about the way we raised them up. Here is the result of the survey.

THINGS THAT I LIKED ABOUT THE WAY YOU RAISED ME UP

- that you raised me with siblings in the house
- that you had Islamic rules in the house since my birth
- that there is no violence in the family
- that there is trust
- that we respect each other's views, therefore get along
- that you raised us with a sense of humor
- that you gave us the reasoning behind all your rules

- that there were set rules
- that you never broke your promises, whether they were about rewards or punishments
- that I was raised with good manners
- that, Islamicly, you gave me all the information needed and let me choose
- that you had no favorites among us, we were all equal
- that we did many things as a family
- that I was allowed to ask about the reasoning behind your decisions and not be in trouble for questioning
- that you were honest to us even when we were kids
- that I could be my true self to you and not put on an act
- that I could talk to you as a friend about things that happened at school and problems with my friends, and that I would receive advice from you, not orders
- that you could always cheer me up
- that you gave me good advice
- that you told us about our homeland and gave us a chance to visit it
- that you instilled respect in us toward our extended family even though we seldom saw them

THINGS I DIDN'T LIKE ABOUT THE WAY YOU RAISED ME

(There were no responses)

THINGS THAT I DID NOT MIND ABOUT THE WAY YOU RAISED ME, BUT I WOULD RATHER YOU CHANGED IT

- that you were busy, I would have preferred that you had set more time to spend with us (not agreed upon by the two oldest children out of the four)

CHAPTER 8

TIPS TO REMEMBER

The following are some more tips to help parents at odd times with their children. Please take note that these tips complement other advice mentioned in previous chapters and are not a replacement for them. We hope that you will find these tips handy when you need them.

- Never threaten to punish a child with something you cannot execute (e.g., if, while you are driving with your children, one of them makes noise, don't threaten him or her by saying, "If you don't stop making noise, I'll let you out of the car and go!")
- Work out mutual agreements to correct each other's mistakes or behavioral problems.
- Do not give in to all your children's demands or threats
- Don't over protect your children
- Appreciate what your children do even if it is not 100% correct. Build on the positive aspects.
- Provide encouragement in every possible way to your children.
- Avoid sources of discouragement
- Good intentions are not enough, seek knowledge and get some training
- Don't use the same method of treatment for all children, recognize and acknowledge the difference between their personalities and ages
- Don't use the same traditional methods that your parents used to raise you without considering differences in the environment or ensuring that these ways have a sound Islamic origin and are not just traditional
- Parents should agree on the *tarbiyah* plan and be consistent with children

- Don't reward children for doing what they are supposed to do or what is considered part of their duties
- Don't be excessive in either reward or punishment
- Achieve balance between love and discipline
- Be firm and serious when instructing your children to correct their mistakes. If you laugh, they will never take you seriously
- Watch out for too many "no's,"

During the process of *tarbiyah*, we will be faced with situations in which we have to oppose our child's desires. Usually, we immediately use "no," which creates a confrontation between child and parent. At this point, our child becomes defensive and starts counter attacking with tantrums, screaming, calling names. Some of them may even challenge us with, Why not?! or You're mean! or I hate you!

What is the solution? Should we give in to each and every request? Of course not, but we can certainly use some positive alternatives such as the following:

1. Giving information (and leaving out the "no"):

    When Ahmad asks, "Can I go out to play with Ali now?" instead of saying, "No, you can't," give the facts, *"Insha' Allah,* we will have dinner in five minutes." With that information Ahmad will tell himself, "I guess I can't go."

2. When possible, substitute a "yes" for a "no":

    When Fatimah asks, "Can I watch Salam's trip?" instead of saying, "No, you have not had your dinner yet," say, "Yes, certainly, right after your dinner."

3. Give yourself time to think:

    When Ahmad asks, "Can I spend the weekend at Ali's house?" instead of saying, "No, you spent last weekend there," give yourself a chance to think. Say, "Let me think about it, Ahmad." This way you take the edge off Ahmad's intensity. He knows that his request will be seriously considered but at the same time you give yourself a chance to think about it.

4. Describe the problem:

    When Fatimah asks, "Dad, can you drive me to the library now?" instead of just responding with "No, I can't. You will just have to wait," describe the problem to her. Tell her, "I'd like to help you out dear Fatimah. The problem is brother Mustafa is coming for our weekly Qura'nic lessons in fifteen minutes."

5.   Accept feelings:

At the playground when Ali says, "I don't want to go home now. Can't we stay longer?" instead of saying, "No, we have to go now!" show that you accept his feelings. Say to him, "I can see that if it were up to you, you'd stay for a long, long time." As you take him by the hand to go, say, "It is hard to leave a place you enjoy so much."

It is proven that sometimes resistance is lessened when someone understands how you feel.

- Don't be annoyed or uncomfortable when your child asks many questions. This is his or her way of exploring the environment.

- Utilize question answering as a way to bond with your child and build a healthy and open communication channel with him or her.

- Teach your child how to ask others questions in a respectful way through asking him questions or instructing him in the right and polite way.

- Don't talk to your child in an accusing way, it is enough to describe the problem to achieve some cooperation. Rather than saying, "How many times did I tell you to put your coat away? You are a bad boy," you can say, "Coats belong in the closet," or "Coats should not be left on the floor."

REFERENCES

Ala'mer, N.K. *From the Methods of the Prophet in* Tarbiyah. Al Beshry Islamic Books, 1990, Arabic.

Ameen, Goma'h. *Call for Islam: Principles and Fundamentals. Alexandria, Egypt:* Al Da'wah House for Printing, 1988, Arabic.

Bedaiwy, A.A. *Reward and Punishment: Their Effect on Children Upbringing.* Safeer Educational Series, *Our Children,* No. 6, 1993, Arabic.

Carner, Marif. "What Your Teenagers Really Want to Tell You." *Readers Digest* August, 1990.

Dreinkurs, Rudolf and Vicki Soltz. *Children the Challenge.* Plume, 1990.

Eyre, Linda and Richard Eyre. *3 Steps to a Strong Family.* New York: Simon & Schuster, 1994.

Eyre, Linda and Richard Eyre. *Teaching Your Children Values.* New York: Simon & Schuster, 1993.

Eyre, Linda and Richard Eyre. *Teaching Your Children Responsibility.* New York: Simon & Schuster, 1992.

Faber, Adle and Elaine Mazlish. *How To Talk So Kids Will Listen & Listen So Kids Will Talk.* New York: Avon Books, 1980.

Imam Muslim. *Saḥiḥ Muslim.* Cairo: Dar Ihyā' al Kutub al 'Arabiyah, 1955, Arabic.

Imam al Bukhari. *Saḥiḥ al Bukhari.* Cairo: Dar al Sha'b, n.d.

Mahmoud, A.A. *Upbringing of Young Muslims.* Al Mansurah, Egypt: Dar Al Wafaa, 1992, Arabic.

Mander, Jerry. *Four Arguments for the Elimination of Television.* New York: Quill Publications, 1978.

Morgan, W.D. and D. Barr-Stewart. "Focus on the Family" *Family Matters,* 1995.

Qutb, M. *The Program of Islamic* Tarbiyah. Vol. 1 & 2. Cairo: Dar Al Shuruq, 1981, Arabic.

Qutb, Syed. *Artistic Portrayal in Qur'an*, Beirut Publishing, Arabic.

Qutb, Syed. *Social Justice in Islam.* Cairo: Dar Al Shuruq, Seventh Edition, 1980, Arabic.

Shadeed, M. *The Quranic Program of* Tarbiyah. Dar Al Tawzi' wa-l Nashr al-Islamiyah, 1989, Arabic.

Sulayman, A. *Role of Family on Children Upbringing.* Safeer Educational Series: *Our Children,* no. 11, 1994, Arabic.

US Government Printing Office. *Television and Growing Up: The Impact of Televised Violence.* Report to the US Surgeon General's Scientific Committee on Television and Social Behavior. Washington D.C.: US Government Printing Office, 1972.

Yusuf Ali, Abdullah. *The Meaning of the Holy Qur'an.* Beltsville: amana publications, 1996.

In addition:

Other hadith collections like those of Ahmad, Abu Dawud, Tabarany, and Tirmidhi.

Readers Digest articles: "Raising Terrific Teens," "Teaching Your Child to Share," "Children Talk About God," "Guidelines for Parents," "New Career Switch to Motherhood."

Chatelaine's articles in *Family Matters.*